This collection echoes the stori... coast to coast. This book will give you ... ... our nation's youth face on a daily basis. It may shock you but may also encourage you to see how God is moving in the hearts and minds of these individuals.

David Alan, Sonicflood

Nothing encourages my faith more than seeing the power of God demonstrated in real life. These real life stories ignited a fire in my soul. This book reconfirms that God is alive and well on the planet Earth. It is a must read for any Christian and a great source of fresh illustrations for anyone who proclaims the Good News.

Ken Davis, Speaker, Author

T. Suzanne Eller is a passionate woman of God who knows the heartbeat of the Christian teen. This latest work is inspiring, convicting, heartwarming, and thought-provoking. My heart and mind cried as I read these true-life teen stories of pain and overcoming. These stories are Suzanne's innovative attempt to answer the tough life questions that teens have, through sharing the true stories of other teens. In my opinion this is the best way for teens to learn—from each other. I am certainly looking forward to more from Suzanne in the future.

Brandon Hill, Christian Teens Guide at About.com
christianteens.about.com

Powerful, honest stories by teens for teens. I strongly recommend this book to any teenager who is seeking truth in their world . . . and to any adult trying to understand that world.

Bill Myers, Author of *McGee and Me, Wally McDoogle,*
Forbidden Doors

I found myself compelled to keep reading and reading to see the results of the story. That's a great sign for any book. The title says it all! It's the real stories that affect us the most . . . and coming from young people; we should read this book and pay close attention!

Tony Alvarez
Pro BMXer and Youth Personality

T. Suzanne Eller's collection of writings from America's youth paints a crystal clear, and often brutal, picture of what our teens struggle with every day. Those of us in the church have convinced ourselves that somehow the "church kids" aren't dealing with the same kinds of issues that other teens do . . . these testimonies prove that many issues that teens face today are universal. This book is a "must read" for all parents and youth workers—it WILL open your eyes to the stresses and struggles of being a teen in the twenty-first century.

Matt Stockman
Matt Stockman Student Ministries

Where was this book when I was struggling as a teenager? Where were the stories that would have brought hope to a young man who thought there really was no hope? Suzanne Eller's new book, *Real Teens, Real Stories, Real Life,* is full of hope that young people need to know is available. As a young man, I struggled with homosexuality thinking there was no way out for me. I always wondered if there were others who struggled like me. The enemy used my loneliness to trap me in depression and despair, but Jesus shattered through my dilemma and gave me hope and healing. Now I get to tell others about all Jesus can and wants to do in and through them. Suzie's book is a welcome tool in that effort and will bring much hope and healing to those who see no way out! Bless you, Suzie!

Dennis Jernigan
Worship Leader, Recording Artist, and Author

REAL TEENS, REAL STORIES, REAL LIFE

T. Suzanne Eller

RIVER OAK
PUBLISHING

Tulsa, Oklahoma

Real Teens, Real Stories, Real Life
ISBN 1-58919-500-0
Copyright © 2002 by T. Suzanne Eller

Published by RiverOak Publishing
P.O. Box 55388
Tulsa, Oklahoma 74155

REAL TEENS,
REAL STORIES,
REAL LIFE

DEDICATION

To Karen Lee Morrison,
my mother and my friend

CONTENTS

Real Quotes

ACKNOWLEDGEMENTS

I am grateful to Richard, who is my encourager and the love of my life. Thank you for shouldering the burden as I run after my dreams.

Thank you, Leslie, Ryan, and Melissa, for living your life without regrets. I only wish I could have said the same. Your faith and walk with God inspire me.

Thank you to Darrin, Mike, and Shana for sharing your stories. Thanks for allowing me to be "Mama Suzie." You have each been a very special part of the Eller family, and we love you.

Thank you, Janet Kobobel Grant, for fulfilling the dreams of writers just like me.

Thank you, RiverOak, for your step of faith in allowing teens to discuss tough issues in the light of faith.

Last, I thank my Savior because He rescued me. I don't know where I would be today if He hadn't heard the cry of a hurting fifteen-year-old.

INTRODUCTION

A teenager once said to me, "It used to be that parents protected their kids from the hard truths of life. Today, teens protect their parents. It's a harsh world out there, and I don't think my mom or dad could handle the things that I deal with each and every day, so I don't say anything. Sharing sex is as casual as giving a friend a back rub. If I'm trying to live my faith and live purely, and that is my reality, how do I share that with my parents? I don't. I simply let them pretend that things are the same as when they were kids."

Life has changed. It *can* be a challenge to live your faith in a society that has changed its perception of Christianity. But I've discovered that God is not afraid of tough issues. Even though the world has changed, God remains the same. He's relevant in a post-modern society. He's real, and if you are discussing the topics—even if they make the blue-haired lady in the pew in front of you blush—God has the answers.

Ten years ago I found out that I had cancer. The news was really bad. I was scared the day I sat in the cancer center to receive my first chemotherapy treatment. Then a nurse named Diane walked up.

She patted me on the hand as she inserted the needle into my vein and said five wonderful words: "I am a cancer survivor." I stared at the healthy, vibrant person who sat in front of me, and hope surged. This was someone who understood. This was a woman who had battled cancer and survived. She had not lost her dreams or her life. She was on the other side of what I now faced.

That's exactly what we have done in *Real Teens, Real Stories, Real Life.* Each of the individuals is in his or her teens or early twenties. They live in your world. They have faced tough challenges, and not only survived, but also went on to pursue their dreams and discover a purpose for their lives.

If I say to you that living a life of faith will make everything instantly, magically wonderful, then I am not telling the whole truth, and I might even be setting you up for failure. But what I can say, and what these stories will demonstrate, is that following Christ is an absolutely amazing journey.

I've read hundreds of stories from teens across the nation. I've wept and prayed for teens who were shaped by circumstances that weren't their fault or who bore the consequences of mistakes that were. Almost all of the teens who shared their stories failed at some point as they tried to find their way to God. Some were spiritually bruised and embarrassed as they tried to learn how to walk in faith with confidence. Others almost gave up but instead picked themselves up and allowed God to help them take the next step.

The questions at the beginning of each story are also real. Teens just like you shared their doubts and the problems that they want to overcome.

"You have no clue what I'm facing," you might say. You're right, but I do know my own story, and I am continually delighted at the plans God had for me even when I had given up hope. This book was borne out of a lifetime of watching God work and understanding the depth of love and purpose that He has for each of us. God was and still is my Cheerleader, even when I failed to believe in myself. He is standing in the background, waiting for me to take the next step and rejoicing when I do.

The combined journeys of faith in this book demonstrate that there is always hope. As George Eliot once said, "It is never too late to be what you might have been."

Isn't that awesome?

I believe in you,
Suzie

REAL TEENS, REAL STORIES, REAL LIFE

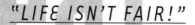

"LIFE ISN'T FAIR!"

ROAD TO RECOVERY

By Jennifer H., Age 19

I could have been described as a pretty normal teenager. I was always busy with school and was an active member of my high school's JROTC program. The rest of my time was spent either working at Subway or hanging out with friends. I loved running, juggling, playing guitar, going to the beach, surfing, partying, and basically anything fun. Although I was raised in a Christian family and had to go to church almost every Sunday, I didn't believe God was real. I couldn't understand how there could be so many different religions and only one true God. I was searching for some rational way to explain things.

Religion just seemed like a nice way to keep society in order. Besides, I was having fun living my life the way I was. Why should I change for just some God that might not be real?

The summer after I graduated from high school was one of the happiest times of my life. I had just turned eighteen. I was enjoying my last easygoing, fun-filled summer days before starting college at UCF. Everything was falling into place. Nothing but promise lay ahead.

All those plans took a drastic turn one hot Fourth of July afternoon. Several of my friends from work and I decided to go to a party to celebrate the holiday. There was supposed to be skiing, volleyball, etc., but when I arrived, everyone was just sitting around talking. I was bored and hot from sitting outside, so I decided to take a quick dive into the lake. I changed into my bathing suit and headed toward the dock.

I had no idea that within moments my life would never be the same.

I remember everything about the dive. I thought it was great. It had great form. Those carefree thoughts were quickly interrupted by a sudden jolt into the bottom of the shallow lake. I remember how unexpectedly my hands touched the slimy bottom. They immediately buckled, and then my head made contact. I heard a jarring sound as my neck snapped. I flipped over and lay facedown in the water.

I knew I had to get out quickly. I tried to swim but couldn't seem to go anywhere. I opened my eyes and saw all my limbs floating motionlessly in the water. I couldn't move at all!

Extreme panic set in. Now, all my concentration was focused on holding my breath. Since I've always been such a prankster, I knew my friends would think I was kidding. The longer I held my breath, the more I felt like I was going to die. I couldn't believe my life was going to end like this! I held my breath until I couldn't hold it anymore. I remember thinking, *Well, I guess this is it.* The water started to seep into my mouth, when finally someone's hands pulled me up and out of the water.

The man who pulled me out of the water was named Kyle Mason. He had made plans to celebrate the Fourth of July with his friends. They came to pick him up, and he was walking to the parking lot, when he had a sudden urge to stay home. His friends were upset at the sudden change of plans, but something told him not to go. After his friends left, Kyle noticed a party going on outside at a nearby apartment. As he was making his way down, he noticed my body floating in the lake and rushed to help.

I believe that God put him there at that moment to grab me before I started breathing water. I've never been so relieved as the moment I gulped in my first breath of air. Kyle laid me down by the waterside and questioned me, then ran to call an ambulance.

When the paramedics arrived, they called life flight. I watched as people stood around me. It was surreal. I couldn't move or feel anything below my shoulders. I tried to imagine spending my whole life paralyzed. Just the thought of it made me want to die right then and there.

My parents prayed with me at the hospital as the surgery room was prepared. Their loving words and prayers were the last thing I remembered for quite some time. I spent nine days in critical condition. My lung collapsed. I developed pneumonia. A staph infection raged through my body. Things were looking very bad. My parents clung to hope, but every day they were told that I probably wouldn't make it.

I was transferred to Atlanta's Shepherd Center, and things started looking a little brighter. I woke up one morning in the ICU. A ventilator tube spiraled out of my throat. I couldn't talk. There was something stuck down my nose, and, of course, I couldn't move. I was still pretty drugged up at that point, so it all just seemed like a strange dream.

As the week went on and the drugs wore off, it became more difficult to deal with the new circumstances of my life. My life had become a horrible dream that I kept expecting to wake up from. But this time the nightmare would not go away.

The first month was the most difficult. It seemed like I had everything taken away from me. It was worse than the most extreme punishment, and yet it was permanent. I lost my job, car, old room, every material possession (such as surfboard, guitars, juggling balls, bicycle, etc.), and all of my independence.

All my dreams for my adult life appeared to be shattered. All my rights as a human seemed to be taken away. I remember thinking, *Why did I try so hard in life just for this to happen to me? Why did I exercise so much just to never move again?*

I started to play a game of "what ifs": *What if I had done a cannonball? What if I had just left the party? What if I never worked at Subway?* The questions were endless and futile.

I wondered what I had done to deserve such suffering. I searched for anything possible that may have angered God. I thought maybe He was trying to get my attention. I promised God I would be as perfect as humanly possible if He would just give me another chance. This phase lasted only days, and then I slipped back into my doubts, disbelief, and questions.

At first I thought I would regain movement. Walking wasn't my greatest concern, but I hoped to move my arms. I could not wait for the day when I would be able to take care of all my personal needs, play my guitar, or just give someone a hug.

Finally I had no choice but to accept the possibility that I might never move anything again. This was undoubtedly the hardest part I had to go through. It was depressing to say good-bye to everything I had ever known. I stared at my old pictures all day, and I cried.

In the middle of physical therapy one morning, the song "Happy" by Sister Hazel filled the gym. Immediately the memories flooded my mind. Everything was perfect then. I was at a Fourth of July celebration watching fireworks, listening to Sister Hazel play, hanging out with all my friends, and having a great time living a normal life.

I wanted to be that girl again. She could laugh. She knew how to have fun. She was happy. She didn't belong in a wheelchair. As the song played, I cried. I wanted my old life back, but as much as I did not want to believe that this had happened, there was no way around it. I had to deal with it sooner or later.

I distinctly remember the day I started to accept my injury. It was the second month after the accident, and I was crying, thinking about what my life had become. Only this time I felt something different. It finally clicked. There was no changing what had happened, so I had to pick up the pieces that I could and move on. I had to stop feeling sorry for myself and try to press forward the best I could. That was the good news, but the bad news was that I stopped crying out to God. I decided to prove to my friends that I was the same person I was before the accident.

Then September 11, 2001, happened. The attacks made me realize how fragile and uncertain our lives are. I wanted to give God a chance. As I sorted through these thoughts, I stumbled across a Web site of a man who had also broken his neck in a diving accident. He shared the peace and indescribable beauty of his short glimpse into Heaven when he faced his near-death experience. As I read his story, I realized that I had found my answer because this man's story made me face my own memories. I suddenly remembered that immediately after I was pulled out of the water, I frantically told everyone that I was lost. The moment I was faced with death,

I knew I had not lived my life for God. The thought of eternity was not peaceful at all.

When I was in critical condition, I had no visions of peace, but rather complete darkness. I was terrified, and all I wanted was to find a way out of my situation.

I knew that it was time to open my heart to God.

I constantly sought God from that point on, and He never failed me when I did. As soon as I understood how real and powerful He is, it was frightening to think about all the sin that was once a part of my life. As I faced God, I shook and cried, but God got a hold of me in such a strong way. There's no other way to explain it. God opened my eyes, and all I could do was crumble before Him. I'm so glad God has given me a new life, one where I look forward to each new day with God as my best friend.

REAL QUOTE

God showed me that He had always been there for me.
He had always provided for me. So why worry and be
afraid now that my circumstances had changed?

—WILL B., AGE 16

MY PRAYER

*Dear Jesus, my world has fallen apart, and I can't find a
way to put it back together. Please wrap Your love around
me and show me that You care. I want to learn to trust
You. I want to take Your hand in the midst of the darkness
and follow in Your footsteps. I can't do this by myself,
but with You by my side, I will find my way.*

*"I STRUGGLE WITH PORNOGRAPHY
EVEN THOUGH I KNOW IT'S WRONG.
I FIND IT ADDICTIVE AND
THRILLING, AND I CAN'T SEEM
TO BREAK AWAY, NO MATTER
HOW GUILTY I FEEL ONCE I DO IT."*

NO WAY OUT

By Darrin B., Age 24

I still remember that night like it was yesterday. I worked at the mall and left around 10:00 P.M. I said good-bye to my friends and headed for the two-bedroom trailer that I now called home. Little did my friends know that my "good-bye" had a whole different meaning. I had decided that I would take my own life, the worst decision of many bad choices I had already made.

What makes a person choose to commit suicide? I was one of those people who said that life could never get that bad, that things could never be so horrible that they were beyond repair. I wasn't committing suicide because my life was out of control, but rather because I was tired of fighting

28

and losing a personal battle. I felt like there was no other way out.

It all started five years earlier. I was excited when I entered the youth group. I was in seventh grade, and my youth pastor seemed like a great guy. He was cool and funny, and he never seemed to mind having teenagers at his house at all hours. The first time I was in his home, I noticed a couple of movies on top of his television. I don't remember the titles, but I popped one in. It was basically soft porn.

Shortly after that, our youth pastor took all of us to a youth convention. One night he assembled the guys together in his room and rented an X-rated movie. I watched, intrigued by what I saw.

From that time on, I was hooked. I lied and deceived to get my hands on pornography. I craved it. Doctors say that the portion of your brain that can become addicted to heroin is the same part that functions when addicted to pornography. They also say that porn is as hard to shake as heroin.

I believe that because that is how it felt to me.

Every Sunday and Wednesday, I heard our senior pastor say that behavior like mine was wrong. I was in total inner conflict. I knew that I could never be good enough to please God, yet I was so afraid of missing God that I continued to go to church.

I was alone. I couldn't tell anyone how I felt or what I was going through. How could anyone understand? I knew that everyone would look down on me. I hated who I had become. I hated me.

Things steadily deteriorated. I moved out of the house when I was only a junior in high school. My relationship with my family at home had not been good for a very long time. I was raised in a "religious" home, but the abuse and words that were spoken behind closed doors were very different from the façade that everyone else saw.

I worked full-time and attended school. I thought moving out would solve my problems, but it just made things worse. I was now more isolated than ever, and yet I had all kinds of friends. Have you ever been in the middle of a crowd and still felt lonely? If so, then you understand how I felt.

I changed churches and found one with caring people, but I still had a skewed view of Christianity. I lived a double life, wanting God, searching for God, and yet hiding my sin from Him.

One night at church, a youth sponsor asked me to move in with her family. I didn't realize it then, but God sent that family to me to be my guardian angels. They let me move in and treated me as if I were a family member. They tried to reach me with love, but I managed to keep a wall up between us.

You see, I was still living my secret life. I didn't want them to know how dirty I felt all the time. I hated the way that pornography made me feel, and yet I was always looking for my next "fix."

Other than that, things seemed to be looking up. I had a beautiful girlfriend. I worked at a decent job. But it was hard keeping the porn part of my life separate, so after I graduated from high school, I moved out of their house and into a trailer.

It didn't take long for things to fall apart. I was caught in more and more lies. I made several terrible financial decisions, and the debt piled up. My girlfriend and I broke up. I felt alone and worthless. I thought the only way that I could deal with this was suicide.

When I arrived home that Tuesday night, I immediately wrote notes to all the people I loved. I made sure every detail was in place. I lived by myself and didn't have to be at work until Saturday. By the time anybody missed me, it would be too late.

It was 4:00 A.M. when I finished my suicide notes. I scrounged a can of cream soda from the refrigerator. I sat in a chair in the living room and methodically divided my pills into three groups of ten. I swallowed ten pills at a time, chasing them with several chugs of cream soda and gagging. Then to make sure that I was successful, I followed that with half a bottle of Dimetapp. I then lay down to sleep.

Do you believe in coincidences? I don't. The next morning at around 11:30 A.M., my ex-girlfriend, whom I hadn't seen in about three weeks, decided to stop by and see how I was doing. When she found me unconscious, she called an ambulance, and I was rushed to the hospital. I don't remember the ambulance. I don't remember the rescue workers digging their knuckles into my sternum trying to wake me up. I don't even remember them putting in the catheter. I just remember sleeping.

When the doctors did all that they could do, they spoke with my parents. When they told my mom that she could see me, she turned to the pastor of my church and said, "I love my son very much, but if he dies, I want to make sure that he is ready to go. Will you go in and pray with him?"

Before my pastor came in, the nurse told my parents that I had a five percent chance of living. If I did live, I could be in a vegetative state because of the damage to my liver. I remember my pastor coming in and saying that he was going to pray with me. I couldn't reply, but he wanted me to pray with him in my heart. I tried with all of my might to make the words come out, but they wouldn't. I felt like I was dead and attending my own funeral.

Shortly after that, my second mom came in to be with me. I remember her laying her head on my shoulder. She started weeping and quietly prayed for me. Though I couldn't say anything and couldn't open my eyes, the tears spilled down my face.

Hours later I woke up. There was black charcoal spewed all over the room where I had constantly puked up the medicine given intravenously to soak up the poison. My room was a mess. My gown was a mess. Once again I felt dirty, as if the mess on the outside revealed the filthiness on the inside.

The doctors said my recovery was a miracle. I left the hospital the next day. I was given three choices: I could be admitted into a mental hospital, I could live with my parents, or I could move back in with my second family.

Which one do you think I chose? I went home from the hospital that day, and I literally mean that I went home. My second family welcomed me back but this time with new stipulations. They would love me unconditionally, but I had to be totally, brutally honest with them. I couldn't hide my feelings. I couldn't mask the battle of sin.

I knew it wasn't an equal trade because they would love me no matter what, but I wanted to be honest with them. I wanted to get better. I was tired of feeling the way I did, and here was a family—a God-given family—who was willing to help me.

Another requirement was that I had to go to weekly counseling sessions with my Senior Pastor. Through these sessions, I discovered that not all pastors are like my first youth pastor. Little by little I progressed. My new family spent a lot of personal time crying with me and praying over me.

Things didn't immediately get better. In fact, they got worse the first few weeks after I left the hospital. The first week I backed into a family member's car. Then the next week my car was repossessed. In spite of these incidents, I didn't feel like I used to feel.

I think it was because I was learning how to be honest. If I felt bad, I had to say that I felt bad. I couldn't put on a mask. If I lied, those around me gently made me speak the truth. It was hard, but soon I learned to be truthful with God, with other people, and with myself. That allowed me to let people into my life to help me and to hold me accountable.

Four years later, I look back and see where God has brought me. Did I get here overnight? No, it happened one baby step at a time. First, I had to be honest. Second, I needed to understand that God had a plan for me. Third, I learned to look at life as a gift. Now I wake up each day, and I know that I've been given a second chance.

There was a time in my life when I felt trapped by my sin. I thought that I could never walk away from the things that were destroying my life. Now I understand God's love because He opened a door for me when I thought that there was no way out.

REAL QUOTE

Have you ever noticed that people tend to put a higher value on objects owned or worn by a famous person? Worn-out guitars used by rock stars or desks used by past presidents are auctioned for thousands, even millions, of dollars. We often make the same judgments about people, but God doesn't do this. In the eyes of God, we are all valuable.

—DAVID R., AGE 18

(Excerpted with permission from
Meditation Warriors Devotions)

MY PRAYER

Dear Jesus, I want to share every detail of my life with You, no matter how ashamed I am. I know that You have plans for me, but I have allowed sin to push me away from my destiny. Forgive me for wearing a mask. Please cleanse my heart today, and help me to be honest with You, with myself, and with those who care about me.

"IF I TELL PEOPLE WHAT I AM, I AM QUICKLY BEATEN INTO PLACE BY THE REST OF SOCIETY."

P. K.

By Jacob P., Age 17

I have been a P. K. (pastor's kid) from the time I was born. I spent a lot of time playing in the halls of my dad's church as I grew up. When my mom brought me home from the hospital, my older brother took one look at me and said, "So when are you taking him back?"

Maybe he knew what he was talking about because I turned out to be quite a rowdy kid for a preacher's son. I'll never forget when I was in the Christmas pageant. My part was to play a shepherd. When I came out onto the stage, I held the sheep on my head and kept it there the whole show. Anything to get a laugh.

When I went to school, I hesitated when people asked me what my dad did. It wasn't that I didn't like the fact that my dad was a pastor, but kids at school mocked my family, God, and me. I almost became ashamed of what my dad did. I wanted people to accept me for who I was, not just as a preacher's kid.

School wasn't easy for a lot of reasons. I liked girls from a very young age. There was a girl in elementary school whom I liked. When I asked her to go out with me, she said yes, but then she ignored me. A couple of days later I walked up to her, and I asked why she was avoiding me. Her response was, "I only said I would go out with you because I felt sorry for you." It's funny how even little kids can make each other feel rejected and hurt.

I decided to leave school, and I was home-schooled for two years. My mom and I didn't really click during that time. I was always fighting with her about what I had to do. Because of my attitude, I was grounded for most of the time that I was home-schooled. It wasn't all bad. Sometimes my mom and I really hit it off and were close, but two years later I decided to go back to public school.

This time it would be different. I dressed in baggy clothes and bleached my hair. I started to hang out with people who accepted me for who I was instead of labeling me as a P. K. Though they lived and acted very different from my beliefs, they allowed me to be myself.

Dressing a certain way seemed to gain respect. The first day of school a girl dumped her boyfriend, and we were together. When I realized that any particular female in my school found me the least bit cute, I went out with her. I quickly gained a reputation as a flirt who was always looking for someone new.

Music opened the door to more opportunities for me. I loved music of all kinds, but most of all I loved listening to and playing the drums. I was a natural, so my parents gave me a drum set for a birthday gift, and I started taking private lessons from a professional. My initial goal was to play in a worship band and to eventually play professionally. I joined the jazz band at school, and people were impressed with my ability. Then I received an offer to play in a punk band. I wasn't thrilled with the whole punk scene, but I stayed in it because playing in a band brought attention and popularity.

We performed for the high school talent show, and the audience loved our band, the Burnouts. Then we started playing at parties, which could be pretty wild. In fact, the police shut down a few. At this point, I was rebelling against God, and I knew it. I liked my new life, and yet I still felt Him tugging at me. I knew that God was waiting for me to recommit my life to Him, but I also wanted to keep the acceptance from my peers that I had worked so hard to earn.

During this time my family and I took a trip to Alaska to see my cousin. I attended church with their family one night. When I walked into the youth group, I was surprised to see how freely everyone worshiped God. The teenagers didn't seem to care what people thought of them. As I watched them worship, it hit me that God was in that room. Away from everything and everybody, away from home, I could see clearly that God loved me with His whole being—not as a P. K., but for who I was.

I bowed my head, knowing deep inside that I needed to deal with some issues. That night I opened my heart and gave my struggle with rejection and acceptance to God, and He touched me.

When I arrived home, I quit my band. Leaving was the hardest thing I've ever done. I called our guitar player and told him that God had changed my heart. I said that if I was going to play, it had to be for God. When I lost my position in the band, I lost my girlfriend. It hurt, but I finally understood that she had fallen for Jacob the drummer, not me. The losses continued as friends walked away, people who only liked me because I was connected to the band.

I started telling people at school about the one true God. I shared my story with one of my best friends who later got so hooked on the Word of God that he knows more about the Bible than I do. I met a girl who loves God. Today, we are striving to follow not only what God wants for us together, but also what He wants for us apart from each other.

I still play the drums, but now I'm playing for my church worship team. I am writing music that God gives me, and one day I plan to lead worship.

Now I don't fear what people say when they ask me what my dad does. It doesn't matter what they think of my family or me. I look them straight in the eye and explain that my dad is a pastor.

In fact, I plan to be just like him in a few years.

REAL QUOTE

Until you learn to believe in yourself,
you can't expect others to believe in you.

—RYAN E., AGE 18

MY PRAYER

Dear Jesus, You delight in me. I am Your creation.
Help me to be who You have called me to be.
Help me to be real. Forgive me for the times
when I have let others influence me.
Forgive me for the times when I have hidden You,
and also disguised myself, to please people.
I love You.

I SEE ME

By Nathan B., Age 19

Lord, I fall back, back to remembrance as I think
   of that
glorious day when You cleansed me,
shook me, and my sin You did take away.

Now my life's desire is to hear those promising
   words as
they fall from my Lord's sweet lips, I listen for Him
   to say:

I see Me, in you as I look in the depths of your soul.
I see Me, consuming your heart as I open the door.
I see Me, in you dancing with praise on a stormy
   night.
I see Me, shining through as the one and true light.

I bask in the glory of Your Love, and I become
   filled with
the wisdom of Your truth; I try my best
to be a replica, to be strong just like You.

So now I long to hear those words, those words of
sweet release.
I bow down in awe as I listen to my Savior say
to me:

I see Me, in you as the glory of My life so shines.
I see Me, reaching through the corners of your very
design.
I see Me, in you faithful and true as you seek My
very desire.
I see Me, in you as a servant willing to walk through
life's trying fire.

"SOMETHING REALLY BAD HAPPENED TO MY FRIEND. HE WAS A CHRISTIAN, AND I DON'T UNDERSTAND! I'M SERIOUSLY MAD AT GOD."

MY BEST FRIEND

By Natalie D., Age 21

Best friends, they seem to come and go throughout the years like the waves of the ocean, here today and gone tomorrow, but the memory of those best friends will always hold you close no matter how far apart you are. Whether it is miles that keep you away or some other kind of change, the memories that you have shared will never disappear.

I realized this at the end of my ninth grade year—a year that sometimes I wished never would have happened, but most of the time I am thankful for. From the day that I received that phone call, I have never been the same.

It was our day off. I was in the process of preparing to go to Target with my mom and twin sister, Abigail. The phone rang, and on the line was

my good friend Cole, who seemed to be laughing hys-
terically. I was in the mood for a good laugh, and I
began to smile. However, as she spoke, I realized
that it was not a happy tone in her voice, but rather a
hysterical one, full of horror and fear. As she tried to
explain to me what had happened, all I can remember hearing were the words "Jacob" and "drowning."

I fell to my knees and began to scream. My mom
rushed up the stairs and grabbed the phone. I
repeatedly cried aloud, "God, don't let him die!
Please, God, don't let my best friend die!" With that
I rushed to the hospital, pajamas and all. Behind the
ominous yellow doors, the stiff white uniforms, and
the blue waiting room of the Intensive Care Unit, I
started the journey into my friend's damaged world.

That moment changed my view of how fragile
life is. What had once been abstract became a
reality as I saw "behind closed doors" of the ICU.

The painstaking process to recovery for my
friend began after the near-drowning accident.
Doctors reported that the lack of oxygen during the
eight minutes Jacob was underwater might leave him
a vegetable for the rest of his life. Before long,
Jacob's day-to-day world was wrapped in tra-
cheotomies, feeding tubes, seizures, comas, needles,
bad news, and more bad news. Jacob was flown to

Baylor Medical Center in Dallas to have tests run on him and, hopefully, to receive positive treatment.

The ways that Jacob's accident changed my life were hard lessons to learn. However, I might have never learned them any other way. In fact, the night before he almost drowned, I remember writing in my journal that he was mean to me. I was jealous of his relationship with my twin sister. He was actually in love with Abigail, and the fact that she could care less about him was almost too much for me. I was willing to do anything for him to treat me like a friend again.

I distinctly recall God speaking to me the night before Jacob's accident. He said that Jacob would not always be there for me. I was thinking something along the lines of him moving away or changing schools. It was not until a few days after his accident that I even drew the connection between what God had spoken and what had happened.

The hardest thing during this time was realizing that in times of trouble, you always go to your best friend to talk. However, my best friend was the one on the hospital bed with tubes in his nose and monitors beeping all around him.

Whom could I depend on, but God? Although it was hard, I learned to trust God more every day. I spent most of my waking hours in the ICU waiting room, and I thought a lot about my friendship with Jacob. I determined that I would stay faithful to him, no matter what.

It's been six years since that first lonely day in the hospital. I've traveled to Baylor Medical Center in Dallas with him three times; sat for countless hours with him; and spent my lunch breaks with him, not to mention weekend time. I still go over to his house and work with him on things like tying his shoes and getting on and off the trampoline.

You might see us walking down the road during our afternoon routine of picking up trash. Jacob has an obsession with trash due to an extreme periph-eral vision problem from the accident. He sees better out of the sides and from beneath his eyes rather than straight ahead, so all the trash is in his view all of the time, and it bothers him.

I can only imagine how humorous it must be to drive by and see a young man, walking with arms straight up towards the sky, giddy as a horse running free; while at the same time there is a young woman, hopelessly holding a bag walking behind picking up trash.

However, it doesn't bother me that it may look funny because I'm with my best friend. I'm with

Jacob doing things that he really enjoys. It's no different than when we used to skateboard solely
because he enjoyed it, or when he would spend hours
with me studying for stupid tests for which he
needed no help, just so I could make a good grade.

One time, during a daily visit with Jacob, I took
him to the store with me to buy something for
Abigail. Since it was a present, I decided it would be
nice to wrap it. As I held the scissors and tape in my
hand, I questioned whether or not Jacob would want
to wrap it for me. The minute I asked, he grabbed
the scissors and cut away with no real pattern at
the pretty paper. Once he finished, he took the tape
and unraveled it for quite sometime before I
stopped him to tell him that he had enough tape.
He just laughed as it stuck to his fingers, my
fingers, and the tape itself.

As he tried to tape the edges of the wrapping
paper together, he got mixed up, said in disbelief, "I
can't do this," and threw the tape to the floor. He
closed his eyes as if the problem would disappear. Of
course, his problem didn't go away, and I was there,
once again, to encourage him to try once more. He
tried a few more times, and the tiny packages were
finally wrapped and ready to give with love. The
beautiful mess that he had accomplished was so
precious that I hated it when Abigail had to tear into

it. Sometimes, it's easy to forget how beautiful a messy thing can be.

Often, you don't realize what you have until it's gone. It's a lesson I would have much rather learned another way, but God's timing has never proven me wrong yet. If anything, in this whole Jacob experience, I have learned what true love is. It's giving. That's all. The greatest thing you can ever give to anyone in life is to give him or her your time. Anyone can give talents, and most can give money, but when you give of your time, you truly reap the benefits of being a friend.

Jacob wrote a story about me recently. It read: Natalie is a girl I love. She is beautiful. She is pretty because she has red hair and is tall. She is my friend. She loves God and goes to church. I hope I marry someone who is tall and loves God. I love Natalie. Not because she is my girlfriend, but because she is my friend.

REAL QUOTE

You're never too young to serve. When I was younger, I always wanted to help out at my church, but I was told that I was too young to be of help. But I know that's not true, there's always some way to serve God.

—CHARITY S., AGE 14

MY PRAYER

Dear Jesus, I sometimes think that if You had been there, things would have been different. Help me to trust You. I know that You love my friend even more than I do. Thank You that my friend doesn't have to face this alone. Thank You that You will help me during this difficult time. Help me to serve my friend with Your compassion and love.

SUNRISE

By Rebekah H., Age 17

She sat and gazed upon the light
Just toward the end of day
Not knowing it would soon be night
No sun to light her way

For naively she sat and dreamt
And laughed away her care
She had no need to weep or cry
Her blessed light was near

But suddenly 'twas cold and dark
The light behind the sea
Had gone to find a resting place
For all eternity

She shouted to the cold dark night
And bid it go away
But even though she wept and cried
She could not make it day

Her light was in another place
Within some hidden land
And somehow she must find the strength
To do the task at hand

And so she labored through the night
She toiled, she worked, and pined
In everything she did and said
The light through her did shine

For deep inside she realized
The light, her blessed friend,
Though from her presence gone for now
'Twas soon to rise again

REAL QUOTE

When I lost Sarah, I asked the question, "Why, God?" He brought me comfort in an unexpected way, through the sunrise. I know that one day we will all rise, and I will see Sarah again.

—REBEKAH H., AGE 17

(Excerpted with permission from *Meditation Warriors Devotions*)

BUTTERFLY MAN

By Brooke S., Age 20

I thought I was losing my mind, going psycho. I never told people what was going on inside of me. I only shared the surface stuff that was evident for all to see. I skipped classes in school because I didn't see the point in going. I laid in bed and blocked my door so my mother couldn't come in. She eventually gave up, but I had already given up on myself.

While I was at home, I started cutting myself. It made me feel better in some weird way. I wrote things in my arm with a razor as if my flesh were a billboard for all to see my craziness. My mother freaked out when I came out of my room with my arms covered in bandages, swaddled under my long sleeves. Then I moved to my stomach because there was more room to write.

My mind swerved from thought to thought, plans of hurting myself to pay back those I loved with pain. I hoped they would realize what they lost and that others would look down on them for not being there for me.

My only outlet during this time of my life was art. It was a passion, and I painted and created projects on the potter's wheel. Ceramics was the only reason I attended school.

Some days I loaded up my easel, paper, paint, and water bottles and drove far away to a wooded area. I walked so deep into the woods that I lost myself in the scenery. Though it was only forty degrees outside, I sat and painted in the middle of nowhere. I was content to be alone with my art. It was calm, and no one knew I was there. I could paint and listen to the stillness that surrounded me.

It was my secret place and there I could be happy—not full happiness, not like laughing, but peaceful. If I wanted to scream, I could. I could yell and cry as loud as I wanted, and I didn't have to explain why.

I became a hermit. Though I didn't talk much before, my silence became ridiculous. The strange thing is that I continued to be involved in school. I was in the marching band. I was also in the Guard, and I took it very seriously. I practiced for hours, building up my strength and tolerance.

I had friends, including my best friend, Christina. I shared with her the details of my life, and she couldn't believe it, but I understood. I had trouble accepting it myself.

At the end of my senior year, I enrolled in college to study art. I traveled to St. Louis with big plans, imagining how I would arrive at this new place and how everything would be great. I believed that my life would be different.

It didn't take long to realize that moving did not solve my problems. I had very few friends. I hated my job, and school wasn't what I expected. I was terribly homesick, not for the "home" part, but for the woods—my place of peace. I drove four hours to Bloomington every other weekend and then four hours back to St. Louis just so I could be in my special place for a few hours each week.

I was miserable at school. I quit my job. I started skipping classes and closed myself away from others once again.

Same old, same old. Back to my previous life.

One night I was writing a term paper. As I sat in front of the computer, I thought about how lame it was that I was doing nothing. I decided to see a movie, so I drove to "The Loop," which is a downtown area in St. Louis.

I decided to burn time while I waited for the movie to begin. I was walking down the street when I saw two girls in front of me. A man stood on the sidewalk and held out a flier. They pushed it away. I marched up and took the flier since those two girls had acted so rudely to the guy. I figured that he was promoting a band or something. I took the flier from him and started to walk away when he said, "May I ask you a question? What is your relation-ship with God?"

I stared at him, and then I laughed because his question sounded really funny. I didn't understand how anyone could have a "relationship" with God! The guy said his name was Jamie, and then he introduced me to another person named Chuck. More of their friends joined us. For the next two hours I stood on the street, and we talked about God.

I couldn't believe it. I was raised as a Christian, but I never felt the same way about it as I did on this night. I looked at each one in the group of people and studied them, wondering what it was that intrigued me about them. There were about six or seven people standing in the cold talking about God. They each seemed to have a beautiful attitude, peaceful and caring.

Jamie rubbed his hands together and warmed them. "Brooke, do you want to accept Christ?" he asked.

"Stop talking to those guys!" someone shouted and interrupted our conversation. I stared at a guy that I knew who stood not far away. He had walked by earlier and asked me to come and hang out with his friends. He was not a good person, and I definitely didn't want to spend time with him and his friends. When I said no, he had waited close by and listened to every word that Jamie spoke.

"Do you want to accept Christ?" Jamie asked again.

Chuck joined him, saying, "It's up to you, Brooke."

"You don't have to listen to them," the guy shouted. His friends joined in and started mocking Jamie and Chuck. My natural response was to yell at him to shut up, but I actually felt sorry for him.

I nodded. "Yes, but will you pray with me?" I asked.

The whole time that I prayed, the guy and his friends cursed me out. I clenched my eyes shut and peace flooded me. The words of those who stood in the background and mocked me helped me to understand what I was walking away from. I thought, *They are still stuck, but I found my answer.*

Soon after I was saved, I found a project I had created titled *Butterfly Man.* It was an assignment for my graphic arts class. *Butterfly Man* had the body of a butterfly, but the face was a composite of several different graphic files of men's features. As I studied it, I almost dropped the piece. The face looked like Jamie, the man who had stopped to share his faith with me on the street. Same goatee. Same face shape and coloring.

Was God reaching out to me even before I met my new friends?

I took the portrait to Jamie, and he framed it. "Isn't it awesome, Brooke?" he said. "Butterflies are a symbol of new beginnings."

There are still reminders of my past. Sometimes if I'm really cold, or if I've just come out of the shower, I can see the faint outline of the word "Why?" that I carved on my forearm. That was a question I asked when I had no answers.

Today it is a reminder that my scars are healed—in more ways than one.

REAL QUOTE

When I accepted Christ, I became a part
of the best family ever. It is a family with
unconditional love—the family of Christ.

—STEPHANIE H., AGE 23

MY PRAYER

Dear Jesus, help me to be still and know that You are God.
Thank You for real peace that comes from knowing You.
You are a Shelter, a safe Place where I can find real joy.
Thank You that You loved me first.
Thank You for healing my scars with that love.

WHO AM I?

By Melissa E., Age 18

I have dreams
That will come true
I have goals
That I will conquer
I have morals
Which will remain pure
I have pride
That I will not let fall
I have ability
That I will turn into strength
I have respect
Which will not turn into rebellion
I have direction
And will not get lost
I have love
That is not bound by race
I have courage
Which I will use to stand up for what I believe
I have a mind
That will not be wasted

Who am I?
I am an American teenager
Whose leaders have given the name
X

I will rise above your standards

"WHY SHOULD I CARE? IT'S NOT LIKE I CAN DO ANYTHING ABOUT IT. IT'S NOT MY PROBLEM."

STRANGERS IN MY HOUSE

By Jamie C., Age 15

I stood staring out the front window of my home. I was sick to my stomach as I watched the kids climb out of the car and walk to the door. I didn't want to talk to them, but my mom ushered me in front of them and introduced us. The lady from DHS stood in the background, watching to see how the foster kids would react to their new home.

The kids seemed willing to adapt, but I started to put up walls right then and there. I didn't want to have anything to do with these strangers in my house. I walked into my room and cried myself to sleep.

It all started when my parents helped a family in the church who was struggling. We took their children in for a short while until the parents got on their feet. That wasn't such a big deal, but I was shocked when my parents decided to open our home to foster kids. Seeing the circumstances of the family from our church had opened my parents' eyes to the needs of other kids who were without a safe place to stay during tough times.

I was an only child and thirteen years old. I didn't want my life to change. The thought of kids moving in with me and rearranging our lives did not sound pleasant. I felt as though my parents were trying to replace me or that I wasn't good enough for them. I thought that God had turned His back on me.

After the foster kids arrived, I did everything I could to annoy them. I knew just what to say or do to make them mad. I disliked them so much that my feelings were at the point of hatred. I was defensive and looked for opportunities to show my parents why this was a bad decision. I prayed every night that God would take these people out of my home and return everything back to normal.

One night I was praying my same old prayers, asking God to give me back my life, when He showed me something. He shared with me that if these kids didn't live with us, they might never have the chance to know who He is or that He loves them. I sat on my bed as God made me face the truth. The kids that came to our home might never understand what it means to be secure. I realized that because they lived in our home, they didn't have to worry about finding their parents drunk or high, and they could feel safe from abuse. I had heard their stories. Some of these kids had faced things I couldn't even imagine, much less live with on a day-to-day basis.

I let the walls crumble that night. I asked God to forgive me. I knew that my parents had enough love for all of us, but what about me? Did I have enough love to share?

God had really softened my heart. It wasn't fun picking on my foster brothers and sisters anymore. One day I had the perfect opportunity. My foster sister had messed up, and if I told my parents, she would be in big trouble. I had compassion for her and kept my mouth shut.

Some of my foster brothers and sisters have been hurt to the point that they don't know how to trust others. Some have been neglected and feel abandoned. Many love their parents but are sepa-rated from them, and they have no idea when they will be a family again. I can't solve those problems, but I can share with them that God loves them and hasn't turned His back on them at all. In fact, He brought them to our home so He could give them a dose of His love.

Am I the same old Jamie? No, and I'm glad. Two years later, I have learned how to be patient with people. I accept life as it comes. I appreciate what I have. I'm thankful for the love of my parents, not just for me, but also for others. I'm definitely not as cranky or as stubborn as I used to be. I'm more open and compassionate toward people and the problems they face. Before the kids came, I had limited vision. I saw the world through my own circumstances. My foster brothers and sisters have helped me to see things from other people's point of view.

Our new family is not perfect. Sometimes I fight with my brothers and sisters, just like everybody else. When a new kid comes around, it takes time for all of us to get used to him or her. But there is one major difference: When I see the stranger walking to the door, I'm there to welcome my new foster brother or sister to his or her new home.

REAL SCRIPTURE

"Whoever welcomes one of these little children in my name welcomes me; and whoever welcomes me does not welcome me but the one who sent me."

MARK 9:37 NIV

MY PRAYER

Dear Jesus, open my eyes. Help me to see those who are hurting. Thank You, Lord, for my parents. Thank You for giving me a warm bed and food and shelter. Thank You for parents who love You, who love each other, and who love me. Forgive me for taking all of this for granted.

"WHAT DID I DO TO GOD TO DESERVE THIS?"

A PLACE TO CALL HOME

By Nichole J., Age 19

What do you think about when you say the word "home"? Maybe you think about mom baking apple pie in the kitchen or warm smiles and welcome arms. Well, when I was about six years old, my dad put me in charge of helping him with our tomato plants. I was so excited, and I watered them every day. I watched them grow green and tall. I went to my dad one day and asked, "Dad, where are all the tomatoes?"

He said, "Don't worry about it. They just didn't bloom right." Later I realized that they were marijuana plants.

I moved around a lot when I was growing up, but not because we liked to live in different places. It was because my parents were running from the police. I remember feeling so stuck, like there was no escape. When I was eleven, my home really fell apart. My dad came to me one day and told me we were getting kicked out of our house.

"Oh, no, not again. This always happens to us," I said.

"No, this time it's different," he said. "This time we don't have anywhere to go." Before, we had always managed to find some family members or friends to take us in to their home until we found another place to live. But by now people were fed up with us.

My parents put all of our belongings in storage and left. At that moment, I knew I was really alone because they left not only the furniture behind, but also me. I was left to survive on my own when I was only eleven years old.

That's when I began searching for a place to call home. I lived on the streets. I also lived from one friend's house to another. I managed that with a little trick I came up with. I would call one of my friends and ask, "Can I stay at your house tonight?" Then I would get there, and I wouldn't leave.

I continued to move from place to place. Sometimes my friends would feel bad that their parents wouldn't let me stay the night, so they would give me the car keys so I could sleep in their car. They just asked me to make sure to get out by the time their parents left for work.

One time I stayed at my friend Maria's. I had been there about two weeks when her mom came to me and said, "Can I take you home? You've been here an awful long time."

I remember turning to her and saying, "I don't have a home, and I don't have anywhere to go." It was the first time that I had actually spoken the truth about my situation. Then I was placed in Child Protective Services, but I ran away from there.

When I was twelve years old, I came in contact with my parents and moved back in with them. One week later my mother was arrested, and my dad was on the run again. The police took me aside and sat me down while they called my relatives. I actually have a lot of family. The police told them my situation and explained that I had nowhere to go, but not one of them wanted me.

I felt like I survived on people's generosity and pity for me. As I grew older, I wanted more than a home; I wanted a place to belong. I would do about anything to feel the security of being someone special. I tried to fit in with the good kids at school, but they rejected me because of my family and my situation. From there I went straight to the kids who were in trouble. I felt I would be accepted, and I was, but there were certain things that came with that package: drugs and alcohol, boyfriends, the list goes on. Still, I chose that route because it came with a sense of belonging.

Then I found a family. I became involved in a gang. I was known as the virgin and faced constant pressure to give in. Finally, one day I decided to do just that. I made plans with my older boyfriend that night, but before he was to pick me up, he and his friends planned a drive-by shooting. He never showed up that night. I was disappointed, and I sat on the couch, watching the 10:00 news. His face flashed across the screen as the newscaster announced that he was arrested for the shooting. I didn't understand it then, but now I believe that God saved my virginity.

One day a friend invited me to a Christian camp. In John 15:4 Jesus said, "Abide in me." The word "abide" means to "settle down and make your home." While I was at camp, I accepted Christ as my Savior, and for the first time I found a real home in Jesus Christ. My relationship with Him is a home that no one can ever take away from me.

After I became a Christian, I changed, but my situation stayed the same. I still had to deal with situations in my life that I didn't choose. A family invited me into their home shortly after I received Christ. They tried to give me everything that they could, but though they were a Christian family, it was not the stable home I had hoped for. They were dealing with their own problems.

There was another family that wanted to take me into their home. They were really different. They were a wonderful Christian family. I loved both of these families dearly, but one place was where I knew God wanted me, and the other was where my heart longed to be. So I kind of lived between the two. It was hard for me to understand why God would place me with another abusive family after all that I had gone through, but God still blessed me in that home. I was homeschooled and finished six years of school in only three years. I was able to leave home when I was sixteen years old and attend a Bible college in South Carolina.

A lot of the problems I faced were because of choices my parents made, but some were due to my own choices. I'm the one who decided to use drugs, to shoplift, and to go along with the crowd when they decided to steal a car. Those were my choices, not my parents' or anybody else's. But I'm holding onto the promise that God has made to me—that all things will work together for good.

I wasn't wrong for wanting a home. No one is. But now I know that it doesn't matter where I go because I can be at home anywhere as long as Jesus makes His home in me.

A PLACE TO CALL HOME

REAL SCRIPTURE

"No, I will not abandon you as orphans—
I will come to you."

—JOHN 14:18 NLT

MY PRAYER

*Dear Jesus, those who should have loved me the most
have actually hurt me the most. I need Your healing touch.
Help me not to be bitter. Thank You for teaching me how to
walk in faith. I pray for those who have hurt me. I pray
that they will see You living on the inside of me. I will
not carry the past into the next generation because
You have given me a brand-new start as Your child.*

*"I SEEM TO BE SPIRALING DOWNWARD.
I'M DOING EVERYTHING THAT I CAN
TO MAKE MY LIFE MEAN SOMETHING,
AND YET I'M STILL DEPRESSED."*

PERFECTION IS OVERRATED

By Samantha H., Age 14

I was seven years old the first time that I felt completely alone. Everyone around me seemed to be dying. In July I lost my grandma. Four months later my papa died. One day after that, my stepdad passed away. My family life seemed to change overnight.

I was depressed, and all I wanted was the attention of those I loved. *Perhaps I'm not good enough,* I thought. Maybe if I took care of the details, I would make everyone proud, and life would be normal again. Maybe this feeling would go away.

When I was ten years old, I moved to my dad's house. I was a top student in my grade, and I played sports and ran for president of the student council. Even though I had all of these things going for me,

I still struggled with feeling worthless. But I did have one person whom I could talk to, my great-grandma. Then she, too, passed away. It seemed as if everybody who got close to me died.

At that point, I decided I wanted to die. Deep down I knew I had lots of reasons to live. I counted them, convincing myself of why I shouldn't die. First, there was my brother. I met him for the first time when I was in sixth grade, and I had only talked to him a few times. I wanted my brother to know that I loved him. Most important, I couldn't bear the thought of hurting my mom and knew the pain she would face if she found me.

I had to make a decision. Live or die? I knew I needed help, but I didn't know where to find that help. Then I made a very terrible decision. I didn't mean it. I couldn't kill anyone if I wanted to, but I threatened someone. I appeared before a judge, and the court system sent me away to Brown's school, a place for troubled teens. The counselors were supposed to determine whether I was violent or whether I had just made a stupid mistake.

Though there were counselors and others to watch over us, I felt unsafe in my new environment. I was surrounded by people who really meant it when they threatened someone. After only a week of living there, I learned a great deal. I stayed at Brown only a week. It didn't take them long to figure out that I couldn't hurt anyone or anything.

I went back to school and quickly found a new group of friends, mostly guys. I was gaining weight because I no longer played sports, and the old feelings pounded: not good enough, not perfect enough. I let my guy friends take advantage of our friendship. They sweet-talked me when they wanted something, like hooking them up with a girlfriend. It didn't occur to me that they only called on me when there wasn't someone else available or when they needed something. I listened as they said inappropriate things. Then one day it hit me: I was the backup girl, the one they called if they couldn't find anyone else to hang out with. My "friends" were using me. It made me feel even more insignificant.

I was going from church to church. I hoped that I could find whatever was missing on the inside of me. I didn't know what it was; all I knew was that I didn't have it.

One night I walked through the doors of a youth church. Before the night was out, I met two new friends, Rudy and Christian. They instantly made me feel welcome. I started attending this church every week. As I listened to the youth pastor, I realized that I understood salvation and that I knew right from wrong, but I didn't have a relationship with God.

For weeks I had watched a room crowded with teens, many of them living for God with everything within them. These teens weren't attending youth so they could play games or join in social activities. They really knew God.

That was the missing piece!

I began my relationship with God. I started reading my Bible and spending time alone with God. I began to understand how God looked at me. It was so different from the way I always perceived myself. Looking at myself through His eyes helped me to accept who I was. I was finally happy with just being me.

I left my old group of friends behind. My favorite quote is "Life is like a coin. You can spend it any way that you want, but you can spend it only once." I have decided that I will spend my time with people who genuinely care. I still struggle sometimes. My friend Christian moved away, and that was hard. I don't like to say good-bye to people that I care about, but even if I lose everything or everyone in my life, I will still have God. I'm not depressed anymore, and I'm happy just to be who God intended.

I still try hard. I still want to do my best, but I'm not aiming for perfection anymore. Being perfect is way overrated anyway.

REAL QUOTE

I thought I had done something bad and that God was punishing me for it. One day I was praying, and God reassured me that He was my Heavenly Father and that He loved me. He healed me of all of my bad feelings. Today I know that I will be used in ministry to help others. I will tell people to never give up because God will help them through the bad times.

—TARA B., AGE 15

MY PRAYER

Dear Jesus, I may not be strong, but I can depend upon You. Thank You for real joy. Thank You for the small things that bring me pleasure that I might have missed. Thank You for the ways You demonstrate Your presence, like in the beauty of a sunset. If You can splash color across the sky, then You can bring joy to my heart. Thank You for loving me.

WATER GLOBE DANCER

By Amanda B., Age 16

She lives on my shelf in a sheltered glass ball.
Her balance is perfect—she never will fall.
Her arms are extended, yet gracefully curved,
Her footing is sure; she can't be unnerved.

Her posture is perfect and sings out with grace,
Her dress is not rumpled; her hair is in place.
In unending circles she dances around.
She never gets weary, although she runs down.

There's beauty expressed on her elegant face,
But her features are hardened and frozen in place.
Her eyes are expressive, and yet she can't feel.
She's perfect, oh yes, but she just isn't real.

Yes, sometimes I stumble, and sometimes I fall,
But I am not trapped in a watery ball.
Perhaps my hair never stays in a bun,
But I'm free to sing, and I'm free to run.

I do not possess that smooth, ivory skin,
That willowy figure, or uplifted chin,
Perhaps I don't carry her charm and her class,
But my life is more than just water and glass.

For, I have emotions and talents to give,
A reason to dance and a reason to live.
I may not be graceful or pretty as she,
But I have a Savior who's caring for me.

He never will judge me if ever I fall.
He thought I was worth it to lay down His all.
He knows what I'm thinking and cares how I feel.
I could try to be perfect, but I'd rather be real.

"WHEN I LOOK IN THE MIRROR, I HATE WHAT I SEE. I FEEL SO UGLY."

GOD'S MIRROR

By AnaLisha A., Age 16

From the time I was in first grade, people have called me ugly. When I entered high school, I hoped it would be different. Surely I would be surrounded by people who were more mature and who would accept me. On the first day of school, I overheard a group of people talking. One guy said that if he were as ugly as me, he would kill himself.

So much for a new start.

Nine years. That's a long time to hear people call you names. When I looked in the mirror, I began to see myself as they did. I started to think about suicide and was very depressed. How could God love me if I was this unattractive?

As I grew older and my appearance began to change, the cruel words finally stopped, but I still felt as ugly as ever. I lived as if the taunts and jokes were my identity. I loved God, and I knew that I was a good person. I cared about people. I had many good friends that I loved and who loved me back. God had even assured me in my prayer time that He was with me. I understood all of that, but I couldn't get past the skewed view of myself when I looked into a mirror.

When I turned sixteen, I had to face hard facts. I had never had a boyfriend, so this had to be the absolute final proof that the words were true. Depression began to creep back in. I knew that I didn't want to go back to that dark place, so I took a chance. I talked to my youth pastor and to some of my good friends about how I felt. They reacted in total surprise. They had no clue that I felt the way I did. My friends helped me to understand that I was looking in the wrong mirror for the answers. I had allowed people who didn't care for me to shape how I felt about myself.

For the first time, I took a long look in God's mirror, and there I was—His child, His creation! God made me the way that I am. He delighted in me.

Today I am truly happy. I will never understand why people are cruel or why they say things that are so hurtful. I'm not sure why I faced teasing for such a long time, but I'm not angry. It's not my job to make them pay for what they did. All I'm called to do is to love them. In my youth group, I look for people who walk through the door with that look on their face—uncertain, not sure if they will be accepted—and I go to them and welcome them.

There will always be those who speak without thinking. Sometimes I feel the thoughts trying to steal back into my mind. When that happens, I push them away by taking a good long look in God's mirror, and I love what I see: His love staring back at me.

REAL SCRIPTURE

The Lord does not look at the things man looks at.
Man looks at the outward appearance,
but the Lord looks at the heart.

1 SAMUEL 16:7 NIV

MY PRAYER

Dear Jesus, Your creation is so amazing! It's as if You took a paintbrush and swirled it across a canvas. You didn't create just one flower, but thousands with every shape and color and scent. You delighted in me as You created me. You picked the color of my eyes and my hair. You shaped my mouth and hands. Thank You that we are each different, each a beautiful work of art in Your eyes. Thank You for helping me to see myself as You do, a work of art created by a Master Potter.

*"IN YOUR WORLD,
GOD MAKES SENSE. IN MINE,
GOD DOESN'T DARE TRESPASS."*

TRIGGER

By Nikki R., Age 25

A few years ago my gang made national news when we went to war with a rival gang. I lost fifty-three friends of mine that summer. I dodged behind cars whenever a car slowed down near me. Sometimes I didn't have time to duck, so I crossed my hands in front of my chest and hoped the impending bullet would miss my heart.

I spent most of my life dodging tough times. I was in state custody for most of my childhood. When I was released at the age of seventeen, I was a time bomb waiting to explode. I immediately joined a gang and sold rock. I had already smoked weed from the age of seven, but soon after I was let out on the streets, my habit was so bad that I sometimes woke up in some unknown hallway, unsure of how I got there.

My whole aim during this time was to excel in my gang, and I did. I planned to be the female president for my block. However, despite the money, drugs, and my friends, I was still miserable. I used to stand across the street from a church and watch as the Christians left the building. They looked happy, and I wished that one of them would tell me what made them so content. I wanted to know how to smile. But no one who came out of the church ever talked to me, maybe because I looked so rude.

Suicide was on my mind all of the time, and I hated my life. I wanted answers, but wasn't sure how to find them. One day two Christians knocked on my door. I was happy to see them, but I didn't let them know that. At first, I tried to slam the door in their faces. One young minister put her foot in the door, and I thought, *She does not know my name is "Trigger."* Privately, I admired her boldness.

I asked them tough questions, thinking I could shake them. "Share your views on premarital sex," I demanded. They answered. I continued to spit questions at them. "Show me where God said, 'Thou shall not smoke weed,'" I said. "Didn't God say the earth and fruit of it were ours?" They answered my questions one by one, but I shot back with more. "How do you know that Christianity is the truth and that other gods are not?"

They told me about Jesus.

I challenged them further. "What color or nationality is Jesus then? How can this God of yours relate to a black inner-city girl like me? What does your God have to do with the people I live among every day?"

One of the Christians looked at me, and she stopped me before I could ask another question. "Nikki, you can come up with all of the excuses and questions that you want, but I want to ask you a question: When you die, where will you be then?" Her voice was gentle. "You know what I'm afraid of? That you'll be lost, without hope, and without Christ."

That got my attention because I knew they were telling the truth about Jesus. I knew I didn't want to die the same way that I lived. I accepted Christ as my Savior right there on my front doorstep.

I immediately started telling everyone about Jesus Christ. Before long, I was preaching on the street corner. For the first time in my life the void was filled, and I had to tell somebody. I had tried Allah, the scientist approach, therapy, hypnosis, and even medication, but I had finally found something that was real. My relationship with Christ filled the void that had been there my whole life.

It is a miracle how God helped me to walk away from my old lifestyle. One day I stood on the street corner, witnessing and preaching. One of my former fellow gang members stood a few feet away, watching. She had come to ridicule me. As she came closer, she asked me about this new game that I was playing. When she saw that I was serious and that I did not curse at her or try to make her leave, she stopped ridiculing me and started listening. I told her about Jesus and what He had done for me, and she broke down in tears, then sobbed. I had the privilege of leading her to Christ that day.

Now every day I pack my ministry bag with tracts, Bible, pen, paper, and New Testaments or books that tell about how to grow in faith. I give away Bibles and books to people who accept Christ. I've traveled with my church on short-term mission trips. I've been in several foreign countries, but my primary mission field is the streets of New York.

I pray before I leave home and ask God to show me who needs to hear about Him that day. Once I arrive, I pray for people to respond to what I am saying. I meet people who are from other religions who have questions about my faith. Others mock or ridicule me. Many genuinely want to know about God and how to know Him. Some ask me to pray that God will help them with their problems. Many accept Christ as we stand on the street corner and pray.

Every day I pray for Christians to understand the need to witness to people like me. There were Christians who never walked across the street when I stood outside their church, but I'm thankful for those who boldly walked up to my door. They were less afraid of "Trigger" than of disobeying God and failing to share with a hurting person in need.

REAL QUOTE

When I decided to allow Christ into my life, I had to think about what I had missed by not having this relationship before. Knowing God would have been a help during those times when I felt so alone.

—VICKI M., AGE 20

MY PRAYER

Dear Jesus, until today, I didn't believe that You existed in my world. Right now I dare to hope that You exist. Please reach down into my life and change me. I want to turn away from the things in my life that have brought me to this place that I hate. I believe that You have more for me than violence and a world of insanity. I believe that You have called my name for a very long time, and today I hear it clearly. Come into my heart, and I will gladly follow You.

TRUTH

By Sandra S., Age 17

I want to escape. I want to get out.
"I can't take this," I say. "Help me!" I shout.
I'm afraid to live. I'm afraid to die.
Afraid to believe, and I just don't know why.
The truth I've found is so real,
Even more genuine than the pain that I feel.
For so long I lived free,
Answering to no one but me.
I can't live this life now that I know what is real.
I'm trying my best, but, man, what's the deal?
Am I destined to lose my life for what's true?
Or am I burdened to live, not knowing what to do?
I can no longer deny the God that I've met.
I'm just a gambler who's lost the last bet.
My heart is aching to be closer to Him;
My body is longing for the world I live in.
The prayers I pray haven't fallen on deaf ears,
But I have ignored the answers for many years.
I'm crying out now, though it's taken a while;
I've strayed so far, my life seems so vile.

The things I praised were not of the Lord;
The things I did He would not have adored.
But now, God, I only want to follow You
And do only the things You ask me to do.

"MY FRIENDS DO THINGS THAT I DON'T AGREE WITH, BUT THAT DOESN'T AFFECT ME."

CIRCLE OF FRIENDS

By Alexandra A., Age 14

I've always been the type of person who needs friends. From the time I was in first grade I had a circle of best friends around me. When I started seventh grade, I met new people. It was fun being together every day. Although my new friends cursed and also teased people in a way that hurt them, I figured that their behavior wouldn't affect me. I thought I was strong. I reasoned that instead of following in their footsteps, I might be able to influence them.

Wrong.

First I said a curse word. Then I started to look at people the same way as they did. I judged people for all the wrong reasons. This new me didn't happen all at once. Rather, I gradually changed as I spent more and more time with my friends.

About a week before my birthday, one person in the group had a brilliant idea. She persuaded several girls to bring Coke and rum to school. This girl talked my best friend into bringing the alcohol to school. They decided to see how far they could take it, and they brought alcohol to school every day and started drinking in secret. One day one of my friends was so drunk that she wandered around our history class, saying and doing very stupid things. Somehow she wasn't caught.

My friends offered me the chance to drink, but I said no. They continued to take risks and drink at school. One day some of the girls were drinking alcohol that they had hidden in a soft drink bottle. A teacher passed by and asked to see the bottle. A girl threw it in the trash can. The teacher pulled it out, smelled the inside of the bottle, and made all of the girls follow him to the principal's office.

The girls who were caught told on everybody, including my best friend who had brought the alcohol the first time. They were all suspended until further notice. The next night their case was presented to the school board, and three people, including my best friend, were expelled from school. The others were suspended for two weeks.

Because I didn't drink the alcohol, I was not in trouble. I was the only one of my circle of friends not suspended or expelled. I felt very alone walking through the halls of school without my friends.

Later that night, I asked God why He let this happen to me. What did I do to deserve having my friends taken from me? Before I was through asking, God answered me. The consequences of my friends' actions were meant to wake me up. I had turned into a follower. That night I decided that I would focus more on God and what He wanted me to do with my life, rather than on what I wanted or what my friends thought.

After my best friend was expelled, I started hanging out with one of the girls who had been suspended. She came back to school after only a few days. We became pretty good friends, or at least I thought we did. That was before all the rumors hit.

My friend was talking to people, telling them that I was saying things behind their backs. The worst part is they believed her. Girls walked by me and called me names. It was hard to wake up and go to school every morning. I didn't know what to do with the time I had on my hands.

I started reading the Bible, especially the book of Psalms. The whole book lifted my spirit. I realized that there were times when David felt alone, and yet he reached out to God. It made me realize that God would be with me as I went through the year without my circle of friends.

My old friends helped me learn a life lesson: It is better to follow God instead of people. I don't have any evil thoughts toward any of my old friends. I have forgiven them with God's help, just as He forgave me.

I have people in my life that I care about, but now God is the center of my circle of friends.

REAL QUOTE

After several months a friend came to me
and asked for forgiveness. I wasn't sure
I wanted to forgive him, until I remembered
how many times God had forgiven me.

—SHELLY S., AGE 16

(Excerpted with permission from
Meditation Warriors Devotions)

MY PRAYER

Dear Jesus, I know that You know what it means to be alone. I realize that many of Your friends left You when You needed them the most. You even reached out and made a friend of the thief on the cross. You were hurting, Jesus. You were abandoned, yet You still cared about his feelings. Please forgive me for caring so much about what others think. You are my best Friend, Lord.

BACKSTABBERS

By Champagne A., Age 17

They smile in your face while they plan their attack
Every chance they get, they stab you in your back
It brings a lot of pain, but don't seek revenge
Put it in the Father's hand; they'll pay for their sins
Because the seed they plant is the one that
    will grow
It's the law of nature, "You reap what you sow"
So when you plan to hurt someone you better plan
    for two
Because the pain you plan is coming back at you
Keep the faith in the Father whom you should
    truly cherish
He will allow the true ones to stand and make the
    false ones perish

> *"THE PEOPLE IN MY CHURCH NEVER GET PAST THEIR PADDED PEWS. HEAVEN FORBID, THEY LEAVE THEIR SAFE LITTLE CHURCH WORLD."*

CHURCH LADY

By Cody M., Age 19

When I was younger, my older brother and I always lay awake in bed, afraid to go to sleep. If we went to sleep, especially on the nights my dad stayed out late and drank, we woke up to the terrifying sounds of my dad beating my mom.

Mom tried to leave him many times. One day she finally succeeded, and as she drove down the road, away from our home and away from the abuse, Scott and I watched our house shrink to a tiny image in the back window.

We lived with my grandparents for a short while until Mom found affordable apartment projects in a nearby town. Mom met and married my stepdad not long after.

Up to this time, our family had no church background whatsoever. It simply wasn't a part of our life. One morning there was a knock at the door. A neighbor lady walked from door to door every Sunday, asking parents if she could take their kids to church. She stood outside and asked if Scott and I could come with her. We dressed in our Sunday clothes, hopped on the bus, and rode to church. For the first time I heard about Jesus.

She came every week after that. Soon she didn't have to ask anymore. Scott and I woke up every Sunday and got dressed and waited at the corner for the church lady to arrive in the bus.

After several Sundays, Scott and I decided to start praying for our mom. We weren't sure what to pray for, so we asked God for two things: for our mom to stop smoking and for her to come to church with us. It seemed like a good place for a six- and ten-year-old to begin in their prayer life.

Our prayers were answered. Mom started coming to church, and the atmosphere in our home changed. My whole family was going to church every Sunday. My mom and stepdad were living for God. Things were finally looking up for us.

Then my dad reentered my life.

My father petitioned the court and gained visitation rights, and now we had to spend every other weekend at his house. Things were very different there. I was exposed to alcohol, cigarettes, marijuana, pornography, and sex. Dad rented movies that kids had no business seeing and asked us to watch them with him. His girlfriend bought us beer. Every other word I spoke was a curse word when I was at my dad's house.

By the time I turned thirteen years old, I had total freedom. I had learned to enjoy the freedom and the things I was doing. For the next two years I lived a double life. I was one person at my dad's home, and I was a Christian and followed my mom's rules at her house.

The visitation rights stopped when I was fifteen, but I continued to live the double lifestyle on my own for the next two years. I took everything I had learned at my dad's to school. My mom had no clue that I was living the way I was. I had become very good at living a lie.

One night an evangelist came to our church to preach a revival. I don't remember the man's name, but I do remember his message. He explained the meaning of discipleship. He said that Jesus desires to have the whole person. He said that when someone gives everything to God, God can take that person to the next step in his or her Christian life.

Instead of responding to his plea to run after God and repent of my lifestyle, I sat. I was angry. I made a conscious decision that night: I would not live a double lifestyle anymore. I would not claim to be a Christian. The hidden, dark side of my life would now be in control.

I left the sanctuary a changed man. I wanted to prove to my friends that I was ready for the next step, ready to plunge deeper into my life of sin. Now I was no longer just experimenting. Sin was second nature. The roles had reversed in my family. My mom and stepdad were now aware that I was in trouble, and they were praying for me.

I was filled with anger. One morning my mom asked me to get out of bed. "I will in a minute," I said. Mom continued to try to get me up, and she nudged me, making me wake up. I jumped out of bed and kicked a hole in the wall and kicked at the door. My mom stood and stared at me, shocked. That night Mom pleaded with me to attend youth camp. "Cody, I really want you to go," she said. "I have the money, and I'll pay your way."

I felt bad about what I had done, and so I didn't turn her down. I left for camp that next week.

Monday night arrived, and the message seemed to come right at me. I was convicted, but I didn't budge. Tuesday night, nothing. *Maybe I can make it through the week,* I thought. Wednesday night I clapped my hands during praise and worship to try to blend in. I slipped to the back of the tabernacle to hide in the crowd. As the preacher gave the altar call, he told a story about friends. He said that if you cared for your friends, you would reach out to them. Two of my friends approached me and asked me to go with them to the altar.

The power of God seemed to be all over me as I stood at the front of the tabernacle. I fought back tears. When the preacher made eye contact with me, I knew I was in trouble. He walked toward me through the hundreds of teenagers kneeling at the altar. Soon I was telling him everything that I had experienced during the last few years.

He placed his hand on my shoulder and prayed for me. Without warning, I was knocked to the ground by the power of God. This was my first God encounter. I came home from camp filled with zeal to change my life. I let everyone know that I was a new person, and I was convinced that this new lifestyle would last.

All through the summer I lived for God. I did all the right things, but I lacked discipleship. I didn't pray. I read my Bible, but I didn't understand it. Slowly I let down my guard. People asked me to go to parties. I tried to do the right thing, but by October of my junior year I had fallen again.

Only this time it wasn't fun. I was miserable. It only took two months to realize that I couldn't continue to live like this. I didn't feel like I had even one good friend. My party friends were there for me when we were drinking and having a good time, but the next day at school they were totally indifferent.

I knew that I had to make a decision. I could either ruin my life, or I could live life as God had asked me. I didn't want to live like my dad. I really desired to live for God, but I couldn't figure out how to do it without falling on my face.

One night I drank so much that I thought I was going to die. I stumbled home after the all-night party. My mom waited for me in the living room and was crying. "Cody, you have to get some help," she begged.

"I want help more than anything, Mom," I said, "but I can't do it by myself. I've tried!"

"Would you try Teen Challenge?" she asked. She sat down with me and told me about Teen Challenge. It was an intense thirteen-month discipleship program.

It was a place where people with life-controlling issues could find hope. Maybe it would help me.

It wasn't an easy decision to make, but as we talked, I knew that this might be an opportunity to find the help I needed. The only problem was that I was only four months away from high school graduation. I would be the first McDonald from the last three generations to graduate from high school. If I left now, I would have to get my GED later.

I sat in my room and weighed the decision. I was tired of living in limbo—wanting to serve God, but living as if He had nothing to do with me. It was time. When I thought about the party friends I was leaving, there was no loss there. I also knew that if I waited, something would change my mind. Some girl might come by, and I would decide to stay and see what happened. Someone might want to party, and I'd be trapped all over again. So I packed my bags and left everything familiar, hoping for another chance at life.

The first day our counselor told us that we would only receive as much as we put in. I tried to make it through the program for the first few days without God. That didn't last long. I needed God, and I knew it. I decided that if God wanted to shake me up, I wanted it. I would completely entrust myself to Teen Challenge, rather than just going through the motions. I would accept what God had for me.

For the next ten months I learned to depend upon God. My relationship with Christ was amazing. I could actually hear God's voice, and for the first time I understood that God had a plan for me.

If it weren't for that lady and her little church bus ministry, I don't know where my family and I would be today. She was faithful. She came to my neighborhood Sunday after Sunday, knocking on doors and inviting kids to church. Maybe she realizes how she impacted the children who climbed on her bus. Maybe she has no idea. I don't even remember her name. I wish I could tell her that the little boy who climbed on her bus week after week found his way. I wish I could tell her thank you.

REAL QUOTE

Some people spend much of their lives searching and
trying to prove God's existence. I know He exists
because I would not be what I am without Him.

—MEREDITH G., AGE 16

MY PRAYER

*Dear Jesus, You sent someone my way! Thank You for
those who were brave enough to risk rejection to tell me
that God loves me. Thank You for every person who has
invested in my life. Lord, use me. I want to tell others
the Good News. Help me to tell someone today.*

"I CAN'T CHANGE THE WAY I AM, AND I REFUSE TO BE A HYPOCRITE."

THE VILE ONE

By Jody D., Age 14

(As told to Penny Lent)

All my life I've gone to church. I was even born on a Sunday. When I was a little kid, I went to Sunday school. I even earned lots of awards and badges, but I only did it to get candy. I didn't give a rip about any of it until a year ago.

When I was in the seventh grade, I was very involved in youth group friendships. I liked the leader a lot, but I went only for the fun. When the leader moved away, I was upset. I didn't know the temporary leader very well, and it seemed the activities had no spiritual impact for me. We had an hour of games, fifteen minutes of songs, five minutes of a "be good" sermon, and then food.

I started asking myself, *What has God ever done for me?* I started to think that if there really was a God up there, then good for Him. Just leave me alone.

I hadn't been to youth group much the summer before eighth grade, so my mom made me go back. I was starting to believe that Christianity was my parents' religion, not mine, and it was annoying to have to attend.

I thought God was lucky to be God. People do such stupid things that He probably sat around and laughed at us. That would make Him sadistic and selfish, as well as lucky. So who needed Him?

During eighth grade I started telling sick jokes and swearing. I got better at it than anyone. I didn't do it at home or youth group because that would mean trouble. Kids at school started calling me "The Vile One." It didn't bother me at all. I even told others about my new title. It kind of built up my ego. I felt different and special.

That summer I met Joe, our new youth leader. He irritated me a lot from the beginning because he wouldn't let me sit in a corner and talk with friends during game time. He made everyone participate. So I started telling him the games were stupid. My buddy and I both complained for the first few weeks, and we were surprised when Joe put us in charge of games.

I didn't admit it, but I felt needed. Later, Joe started a leaders-only Bible study each week, and I liked being included. The Holy Spirit began to teach me, and I actually started following Christ that year. Then God began to impact me spiritually through music. The narrator on the DC Talk album *Jesus Freak* really hit home with me when he said, "The greatest single cause of atheism in the world today is Christians who talk about Jesus with their lips, then walk out the door and deny Him by their lifestyle."

That is true. It seems that faith means little to most of the teens I know who have been raised in a church, just as I once was. I guess going to church is all they've ever known. Among my friends, faith means more to the ones who have recently made a decision to believe in Christ as well as to those who weren't raised in Christian families.

One night in Bible study I read Paul's words in Ephesians 4:29, "Do not let unwholesome talk come out of your mouth." NIV I knew that I needed to clean up my language, so I prayed for God to change me. I read my Bible, and I prayed. I started to learn how to use other words to express my frustration. As time went on, it became easier. Gradually, I was becoming someone totally new!

Sometimes I still have to think about it before I speak, but now my words represent who I am—a child of God.

No one calls me vile anymore.

REAL QUOTE

Let's say that God was the color blue.
Every aspect of your life should
then be some shade of blue.

—KEMISHA N., AGE 17.

MY PRAYER

Dear Jesus, I'm not happy with the words that I hear when I speak. I want to be more like You. I don't want my words to hurt others. Lord, when people see me, I want them to recognize that You live inside of me. Help me to think before I speak and to share the message that You still change lives today.

"PUTTING ON A SHOW, ACTING LIKE I'M OKAY. I'M EMPTY INSIDE."

HOLLOW MAN

By Manny D., Age 24

I counted out the bullets—one for my ex-girlfriend and one for each of her friends. The lyrics of Tool pounded in my head, dancing in rhythm with the hatred seeping through my veins. If the test came back positive, they died. If it came back negative, they lived. It was as simple as that.

If only my life were that simple.

My parents divorced when I was born. My dad was convinced that I was born as a result of my mom's unfaithfulness. My mother tried in vain to convince him that she was innocent of his accusations, but eventually the marriage failed. We moved in with my grandparents who were ministers. In spite of my grandparents' influence, my mom started partying a lot. I remember spending a lot of time sitting by the window crying, waiting for her to come home.

Mom remarried, and when I was twelve years old, she gave birth to twins. Her husband was there for his kids, but he was not a presence in my life. I had no father figure and started to feel like the mistake my biological father had said I was.

My whole life seemed to be wrapped around the twins. They were my responsibility. I took care of the house and the twins. I picked them up after school when they were older. I worked my school schedule around them. With all the responsibilities on my shoulders, I couldn't keep up in school, and I failed my sophomore year.

About the time I turned sixteen, my mom started attending church. Even though she was changing, it was too late for our relationship. We couldn't see eye to eye. I threatened to leave, and my mother made that threat a reality by kicking me out.

I befriended a guy who worked at the front desk where I was a lifeguard. I moved in with him, his sister, and his mom in their flat in Manhattan. I completely dropped out of school and went to work full-time to support myself. Then my friend's mom moved to Oklahoma. She had a business there. My friend suggested we join her, so we packed up what we could in the car and left.

Once we arrived, I moved in with my friend. Then my friend decided to leave for Florida, and for the first time in my life, I was totally on my own. I met a girl during that difficult time. Her parents were preachers, but she wasn't a Christian and was as rebellious as I was.

When we broke up, I discovered that my ex-girlfriend had been cheating while we were dating. The clues were there the whole time, but I had ignored them. Our friends had known, but they felt loyal to her because they had known her much longer than me.

I went to the doctor to be tested and found out I had gonorrhea. The results of the next test, HIV, came back negative. The doctor stressed that the initial result was not always accurate, and that a secondary test would be taken six months later. This test would reveal the true results.

As I waited, I had nightmares of living with HIV. I blamed my ex and her friends. I took no responsibility for my part. Night and day I listened to my favorite band drill their vehement anti-God lyrics into my head, and I seriously started thinking about death. I became introverted. I stopped eating. I sat in my room and counted down the remaining days with bullets.

I had met a friend during my six months of waiting. She was a co-worker and a Christian. She reached out to me and talked to me about God. I laughed at Marci, but she didn't give up, and soon we became good friends. As time went on, I fell in love with her. It was as if there were two sides to me—the dark side who hated my ex-girlfriend and her friends and the part of me who loved Marci.

Marci encouraged me as a friend until the day she left for Bible college. I started to bargain with God once she left. I told God that if the test results were negative, I would live for Him. If they were positive, I would kill my ex-girlfriend and all of her friends.

I had attended church with Marci a few times before she left for school. She asked me to go, and out of respect for her, I did. I felt as if people met me with reproach. I wasn't sure if it was because of my appearance or the fact that I came from New York. I thought that maybe the sin simply dripped off of me and my secret plans were apparent to all. I continued to go to church even while I planned my ex-girlfriend's death, but church had no effect on me whatsoever.

The night before I was to find out the results of my tests, I had a vision. In the vision I was engulfed in silky, ink-black oil. The fingertips of my left hand were the only parts of me that were not submerged.

A thread of light stretched from the fingertip of one finger to Marci, who was walking toward the cross.

I went to the youth pastor and asked him to pray for me. I tried to explain the battle between the darkness of my soul and the light. I didn't share my plans for my ex and her friends. The youth pastor listened, his eyes wide. He immediately prayed for me, but again I felt nothing.

The next day, I waited in the doctor's office. I couldn't believe it when he told me that the test results were lost in the mail. He asked me to come back in one week. Later that day I sat in my room. I was consumed with anger and hatred. I held a letter in my hands from Marci, and in it she encouraged me to trust in God.

I couldn't. Thoughts of suicide were so strong, but hatred was stronger. How could I trust in God? I couldn't even die by my own hand until I killed my ex first. I searched for the gun, but I found out that my ex's dad had come and taken it because it was his. He had lent it to me for target practice and thought I was through with it. The loss of the gun destroyed my plans for my ex and her friends, but I decided I would still kill my ex. It had come down to just her and me.

The next week I waited in the clinic. The results were in a file cabinet, but they couldn't find the key right away. I threw a chair across the room, screaming that I had to have the results. The doctor sat down. "Settle down," he said. "The results are negative."

I ran out of the clinic and fell to my knees. I was bawling, and I asked for forgiveness. I can't explain why or how God reached out to me because my heart was so intent on murder, but He still extended mercy to me anyway. It's the power of forgiveness; evil had to leave when mercy entered my life. I invited Christ into my life, and He accepted the invitation.

I called Marci to share the news, and she was elated. For the next year I wrote to her while she attended Bible college. She encouraged me as I started throwing away the junk in my life. Alcohol was the first to go; I wanted it out of my life. Then I eliminated pornography—my magazines and movies. I began to replace my foul language with words that told others about God and what He had done for me.

Then there was my music. When I was not serving God, I traveled across the nation to Tool concerts and filled my soul with their lyrics. Now I wanted to share my songs about God with others. I felt the call of God on my life in music ministry, and I joined a Christian band as a vocal singer. Singing to God was my way of worship. When I sang to and for

Him, I felt anointed and spiritually fulfilled as if I were exactly where God intended me to be.

When Marci came home from college, she found a different Manny. Our close friendship rekindled, and then the day came when she fell in love with me. I proposed to her, and she said yes!

Now I have started a band called "Krisillis." A "chrysalis" is the cocoon in which the caterpillar lives before becoming a butterfly. I'm in the chrysalis stage of my life—in a state of continual metamorphosis. I will never attain perfection here on earth, but God can use me to influence others while He molds me into what He desires me to be.

One day when I die, I'll become a new and beautiful creature just like the butterfly, but for now I simply want to sing for Him.

REAL SCRIPTURE

"The truth will set you free."

—JOHN 8:32 NLT

MY PRAYER

Dear Jesus, I don't feel that I deserve Your mercy, but Your Word says I can find freedom. I want to put the past behind me. Please help me to start over. Forgive me of my sins. I believe that You are God, and I ask You into my heart today. Thank You for a new beginning.

HOLLOW MAN LYRICS

Words and music by Manny D.,
Lead Vocalist, Krisillis

Verse 1

Here I go my friend, down this dark path again
I can't see the end, but it's closing in
On my mind and soul, I've already lost control
So how can this be, when He lives in me!

Chorus

I was hollow, but then I hung my flesh from the
gallows—
Hollow! Until I hung my flesh from the gallows!
(2x)

Verse 2

I never thought I'd be this gone,
How I got here, thoughts were wrong
I can't tell whose voice is real or fake,
Better figure it out before it's too late
I can't tell whose voice is real or fake,
I better figure it out for my soul's sake!

Bridge

See me as I am
Alone and now a broken man
This could be my end
As I near the bend
Tired of these games I play
I've got one more thing to say . . .

Chorus

I was hollow, but then I hung my flesh from the
gallows—
Hollow! Until I hung my flesh from the gallows!
(2x)

"WHEN I REFLECT ON MY ACTIONS AT THE END OF THE DAY, I FEEL SO GUILTY, SO TWO-FACED."

BETWEEN MY TWO WORLDS

By Carrie R., Age 16

I used to be what is commonly referred to as a "church brat." In fact, I was in church from the time of conception. I grew up to believe that if I acted a certain way and attended church, then I was all right. Church was a weekly habit for me. I heard from others about the joy of a changed life. Some even said that when they accepted Christ, it was the best moment of their life, but I never felt it.

When I was thirteen, I started having trouble in school. I fought with my parents constantly. I liked this guy, but he used me. Then I lost two friends—one died in a car wreck, and the other walked away from our friendship.

One summer our youth group attended an awesome revival in another city. I went to the altar thinking I would find what was missing in my life, but

I didn't. I wondered if God had any use for me anymore. Before long, the sadness I carried around with me turned to silent bitterness.

Over the next two years I developed quite an attitude. I missed church whenever I had the opportunity. I hated nearly every moment of the youth service when I had to go, but I put on a fake smile and claimed I was okay. The truth is I was lying through my teeth. Alone, I would sit and curse myself. I started wearing a lot of dark clothing and black nail polish, and I listened to music that echoed my thoughts.

I didn't like people at all, and I seized any moment when I could surround myself with silence. I started reading books about witchcraft. A buddy of mine was a witch, and I asked her how to cast spells. The whole time I was involved in witchcraft, I also showed up for church activities and Teens-4-Christ at school. I seemed to be in a constant blur, torn between my two worlds.

The summer of 2000, I pleaded with God, saying, "Please come back into my life. I'll try harder!" I suppose God knew what was going to happen—that I would fail Him again because I thought I could do it by myself. I tried to be somewhat different. I attended church more. I prayed a little more. I got rid of the dressed-in-black image and attempted to leave the dark thoughts behind. But whatever I was doing didn't seem to work.

Then came my next battle: hormones! I had never really had a thing for guys before, but when I turned fifteen, my mind seemed to always be in the gutter. The very mention of a filthy joke sent me into fits of laughter. The sight of an attractive guy made my heart pump into overtime.

I was drawn to this one guy. We ended up going out, but not in the best way. Some of our phone conversations and notes should have never occurred. What was weird was that while he wanted to grow in God, I was satisfied being lukewarm.

One day he ended the relationship. He told me that God led him to do it. I was deeply hurt and angry, but there was nothing I could do about it. One month later he called. He wanted to try to get together again, but this time with Christ as part of our relationship. Too bad for him, he caught me in the worst time imaginable. I didn't care about life. I didn't care for anyone. I didn't trust anyone. So we renewed our relationship based on his hopes and my apathy.

Less than two months later the same old temptations plagued us, and he broke up with me for the last time. He said that God couldn't honor

our relationship as it was. Crying and protesting, I
let him go.

One of my friends at school, Tiffany, introduced
me to a girl named Stephanie. Stephanie was a grade
ahead of me, and we were in band together. On the
first day of early band, Stephanie and I sat together.
I noticed something different about her, but I could-
n't really put my finger on it. As the year progressed,
Tiffany, Stephanie, and I became close. Stephanie
asked me to join her and Tiffany at church.

Now you have to understand that I had heard of
this church. People thought of it as a place for the
"elite holiness." These people weren't content to
simply attend church; they lived what they believed.
I lived under the illusion that this church was only
for the best and the holiest people, that someone
from a smaller and not-as-on-fire church like
myself could never be accepted there as a member. I
envied their faith but figured I could never live up to
their standards.

Stephanie didn't give up on me. After several
invitations, I finally accepted and went with her to
church on a Wednesday night. The pastor wasn't like
any youth pastor I'd ever seen, with his casual
attire, spiky blond hair, and even a goatee. I was
somewhat confused when church began and was
puzzled all through the service. This was not the

usual youth church meeting. People worshiped God as if they knew Him. The whole time my mind was thinking, *What are they doing? Why did they say that? Huh, I've never felt this before.*

When the youth pastor asked people to come to the altar, the self-righteousness and pride that told me earlier not to make any moves and not to wimp out snapped. I knelt at the altar, and tears poured down my face. I shook as I experienced God. I felt a wave of peace wash over me.

At 8:46 P.M. on a Wednesday night I rededicated my heart to the Lord. This time it meant something, and it wasn't out of guilt.

I fell flat on my face more than once after that night. I got a too-big crush on a guy. I knew he wasn't where he needed to be with God, but something in me said it was okay. I should've ignored that little something. I ended that relationship in less than a month, and it was a relief.

I made a commitment to God after that mistake. I was tired of taking chances, so I promised not to go after any more guys for a while. I decided to wait until God sends the one He's chosen. I pierced my right ear, and I wear only one earring as a symbol and reminder of this promise. When God sends His chosen partner for my life, then I'll either take out the earring or get my left ear pierced. So if you see me now, look for that one earring. It is my oath to God.

Now I'm growing in Him. Through the help of the Holy Spirit, I'm learning to trust God and others. I'm healing. I've given up my old habits. My mind is clean. I listen to music that lifts up Christ. I feel His love, and I'm not afraid to praise Him. I'm not a "church brat" anymore.

I'm a believer.

REAL QUOTE

Look at us! We use God like weed, just enough to get a spiritual buzz, a religious high. We forget that the Spirit calls us to obedience, to action, and, yes, even to that dreaded word of discipline. See, we get so caught up in the freedom of Christ, we forget that we're also His slaves. And on the flip side, we get so caught up in rituals, we forget the meaning behind it. We reduce Jesus to a gold-plated crucifix on a chain, to the point where we can't even tell you the way to salvation without breaking out the hymnbook to look up "Amazing Grace." We have all faith, but no application. We have all discipline with no meaning behind it. And, ya'll, that's a sorry state to be in. I just want to know. Can we get back to something real?

—LAURA S., AGE 16

MY PRAYER

Dear Jesus, help me to seek a love relationship between You and me. Thank You that I can look to You to find true love, lasting love that is pure. Thank You for wanting the best for my life. Lord, give me a hunger to read Your Word and to pray because it is in those times that I grow close to You. I love You.

SENSES

By Carrie R., Age 16

I can hear . . .
the small, still voice
I can feel . . .
Your warm, calm embrace

I can taste . . .
the cool, sweet waters
I can see . . .
Your loving face

Be with me
Love me
Hear me, Lord
Don't take away the peace . . . within

Let me feel
Let me hear
Let me taste
Let me sense

Let me forever see
and be . . .
with You.

A FATHER'S LOVE

By Jennifer F., Age 19

God has initiated a love relationship with me since I was a child. I remember reading a children's Bible, all seven hundred and something pages, and thinking about who God is. In spite of this I never considered getting to know Him, loving Him, or growing closer to Him.

Maybe it was hard to accept God as my Father because I never had a father. My dad left all four of his children on the West coast and moved to Arkansas when I was only three years old. My mom struggled financially and emotionally throughout my whole life, and because of her own hurts, she rarely talked about spiritual things. My sister had a baby at the age of seventeen, and that was one more addition to our poor family. My sister ran away from home shortly after that, and we've never seen her since.

When I was in the eleventh grade, I sat in a biology class. I couldn't concentrate on the lesson because all I could think about was how depressed I was. Mr. Haines, my teacher, was reading a book on creationism versus evolution. I had noticed that there was something different about this particular teacher. I took a chance and wrote him a note explaining that I was lost. I begged for help. "I want to die," it read. "Tell me what you have that gives you so much joy."

He brought me a Bible and gave me my first Bible verse, Proverbs 3:5 NLT: "Trust in the Lord with all your heart. . . . " That is what I needed to do, but there was a problem. My entire life I had depended upon science, evolution, and theories. I asked God to show me the answer and to give me proof that science was not the truth. I also asked for Him to help me to trust in what I could not see.

The following Tuesday I went to church, and the youth service was canceled for a special sermon. A man who had been an atheist for most of his life shared his testimony. He shared how evolution is a theory and then went on to explain how God created us. As he shared facts, he demonstrated how science backed up a living God.

I was convinced.

Even with my new beliefs, the change of heart lasted only three months. I left my hunger for God behind and replaced it with relationships with guys. I couldn't seem to let go of the sexual sin. I met my first real boyfriend my senior year. He seemed so amazing. He was patient, kindhearted, loving, and treated me well. However, our relationship was less than Godly. When we broke up a year and a half later, I was completely broken.

I turned to a loving Creator. I realized that I could either walk with Christ or struggle with life alone. I chose to walk with the Lord. It hurt. I felt as if God had taken away my joy. I grieved over the loss of my boyfriend, but then I realized that I had to put aside my fantasy world of being with him and instead trust God. Being alone brought good things as well. It allowed God to pluck things out of my life. God helped me to see myself from His perspective for the first time.

Trusting in God has taught me many lessons in the last two years. I have learned that when my family failed me, God gave me a church family. I have realized that although I didn't have a father to guide me as I grew up, my Heavenly Father was and is always near. The difference now is that I recognize Him and reach out to Him. My earthly father may have abandoned me, but I am continually embraced by my Heavenly Father's love.

REAL QUOTE

I'm just beginning to learn from my mistakes.
I now know that I don't want to do anything I will
regret later. If I have sex with someone,
they walk away with a part of me.

—BRITTANY D., AGE 14

MY PRAYER

*Dear God, there is a hole inside of me that I fill with all
the wrong things. Your Word says that I am valuable to
You. It says that You can see the hurts of my heart and
have compassion. Help me to turn to You when I hurt.
Let me find my self-worth in Your presence.
Thank You that You are my Heavenly Father.*

> *"I HAVE FRIENDS WHO WRECK*
> *THEIR NEW CAR, AND THEIR*
> *PARENTS GIVE THEM ANOTHER ONE.*
> *I'M HOPING MY MOM GETS PAID*
> *THIS WEEK SO WE CAN EAT."*

ALL STAR

By Robert H., Age 23

My dad came back from the Vietnam War all messed up and crazy. My mom divorced him. She was fighting her own battle and losing it. My mom had a disease. She was a junkie and lied all the time. Random people marched in and out of her house and in and out of our lives. My mom was away from home when we needed her, but I knew that she loved me.

Many times our refrigerator was bare. We were on welfare, and at times that caused me incredible embarrassment. I learned very early to work hard because we never had money, and I hated being on welfare. I have had a job as long as I can remember. I worked at a pizza place, mowed lawns, tore apart engines, sold candy door to door, worked at a laundromat, and worked at a shoe store—anything to bring in earnings for our family.

I also worked hard in my personal life. I loved playing ball and practiced constantly. Soon I was playing on the All-Star team. When I was in sixth grade, my stepfather died of an overdose, and this caused my mom to fall into severe depression. We were evicted out of our apartment, and we moved into a homeless shelter in San Rafael, California. There we lived in one room.

No one at school knew my circumstances. One day a coach gave me a ride home from a game, and he wanted to walk me to the door. I was horrified, afraid that he would realize how poor we really were.

We moved again. This time we moved in with mom's new boyfriend. They were both junkies and never home. I was totally alone because my brother had stayed behind to live with a friend. I took care of myself. I was very angry when I realized I was taking care of others as well. My things began to vanish—my clothes, baseball cards, and CD player. The refrigerator was always empty. We ate what Kentucky Fried Chicken threw out.

When I was in high school, my mom entered a program to get help with her addictions. I moved in with my godparents, and things finally began to change for me. I could glimpse a future ahead of me. I was dating a beautiful girl. I had tons of friends and was popular among the other students. Very few people realized how messed up my home life and mom had been. No one knew what I had lived through.

I was playing varsity football and was the captain of the Hayward football team. A pastor invited our entire team to a dinner. After the dinner, a preacher was supposed to talk to the team. I only went because of the free food.

I had never really set foot on any church property before. Growing up in a nonreligious home with a drug addict for a mother and an absent father left some big holes in my life. I didn't feel like I was a bad person. All I did was live a typical teenage life: drinking, partying, and dating. But I also felt this huge void. Everything that I had didn't seem to fill the empty space inside of me.

When I walked into the sanctuary that evening, I was blown away at the sight of two thousand students worshipping a God I did not know. Some had their hands in the air, and others were crying. The music was powerful.

I didn't understand it all, but I knew that I wanted what they had. When the speaker preached, he told the crowd exactly how to become a

Christian, and I felt as if he were talking directly to me. The moment he gave an invitation to receive Christ as Lord, I jumped out of my seat. With tears in my eyes, I walked to the front of the sanctuary with a group of football players. I felt a huge burden lift off my shoulders. For the first time in my life, I understood that Christ died for me and took away my sins on the cross.

I didn't understand how to live for God right away. In fact, it took about a year of attending youth group, reading the Bible, ending bad friendships and relationships, and attending church before I completely understood what it meant to give my heart and life to the Lord. I desperately wanted to live for God.

I had always worked very hard for everything that I had, but I couldn't seem to work for this. I couldn't do it on my own, but I kept trying, and I kept failing. One night I was at a drug dealer's house. I was smoking weed with some friends. I was also drinking, so I was totally intoxicated. I was so high that I stumbled outside into the night rain and fell face flat into the mud. The world seemed to spin around me. I cried out to God, "Help me, Lord. I don't want to live like this! I'm tired of playing games. I'm tired of living for foolish things."

The next morning I climbed out of bed and committed to God right then and there that I would give my life fully to Him. I started to read the Bible and was hungry to know the truth. I attended church and youth group every time that I could. I asked God to help me. I'll never forget the day I stood with four of my closest friends and was baptized. It was in a lake by the church, and hundreds attended.

I was a new man by my senior year in high school. I wanted to minister to others, and God helped me to do that. I was on the church high school leadership team. I started traveling on short-term mission trips. Through all of this, I learned how amazing it was to lead others to Christ. At school my friends noticed, and I went from Mr. Party Boy to Mr. Church Boy.

Now that I have graduated from college and am currently ministering to students, I keep in mind that we never really know what the people around us are facing. They may look as if they have it all together, but in reality they may barely be making it from day to day. I have realized that I don't have to earn God's love. He freely offers it to us. When you accept that gift, He can take your life, no matter how humble your beginnings or how difficult the circumstances, and help you become a winner.

REAL QUOTE

Although life may not always make sense
to us sometimes, I know there's
Someone far greater out there watching over us.

—JENNIFER H., AGE 19

MY PRAYER

Dear Jesus, I feel as if I have to earn Your love and acceptance. When I fail, I want to give up and walk away because I am ashamed. Help me to get back up. Help me to learn from my mistakes. Thank You that I can come to You freely and ask for forgiveness and for help. I promise not to give up because You do not give up on me.

SEED, A LOVE LETTER FROM GOD

By Erin Danielle C., Age 14

When you said this isn't working
My heart, it simply sank
My eyes filled with tears
Though you asked Me not to cry

I have to tell you something
Something deep, inside both you and Me
See when you weren't looking
I slipped a seed, a part of Me, in you

It became My mission
To remain in your heart
That was My plan
From the very start
This statement, I hope to be true
That deep down inside
I will always live in you

"THOUGH I GREATLY RESPECT THE TEACHINGS OF CHRIST, I DON'T THINK MY SOUL NEEDS TO BE SAVED BY ANYONE. ALL RELIGIONS LEAD BACK TO THE SAME EMPTY CONCLUSION."

CULTURE SHOCK

By Jessa W., Age 17

I checked my e-mail. It read:

Fwd: CultureShock: Lions, Tigers, and Bears 7/7/99

Fwd: CultureShock: The Ten Commandments 7/8/99

What's all this? I asked myself. I wondered why my friend sent these e-mails to me. *These are all about God. Melissa knows I don't believe in God and that I don't want anything to do with Him. So why is she sending these to me?*

I read them with disinterest at first, but the more I read, the more I discovered all kinds of flaws in the articles. I wondered how anyone could believe this stuff. The "Rob" guy who wrote them droned on and on about how humans are somehow more important and special than any other species. Then something he wrote really made me angry. He said that the public posting of the Ten Commandments should be allowed and that this would somehow benefit society.

I totally disagreed with this guy. He insulted me, and I determined to prove these Christians wrong. Where should I start? I didn't actually have any facts. All I knew was that I was right and that Christianity was definitely wrong. Haphazardly, I started attacking the articles one point at a time, using a premise of confusion to point out flaws in the logic.

As time progressed, I constantly e-mailed two of Melissa's church friends, Jillian and Eric. They let me jab them with my pointed arguments against their religion and gently nudged me with questions about my lack thereof. I cleverly avoided their questions. Whenever they beat me on an issue, I promptly dropped it and came up with a new question to illuminate the faults in their beliefs. Life dragged on through my sophomore year. I continued to ask skeptical questions with underlying cynicism: The world was an awful place full of awful people (except for me, of course).

I hated life. It was depressing, and I didn't want to live in it. If I had to live, I wanted to start over. I wanted something to believe. Christianity wasn't an option, so I searched and found Wicca.

Wicca was a quick fix to my problems. I was ecstatic at having found an answer. Learning all its intricacies distracted me from my sadness. I proudly presented my new discovery to my friends as the perfect way to explain the world and life. But as our religious arguments continued, I realized that Wicca, with all its tree worshipping and detailed ceremonies, wasn't an adequate explanation of the universe.

I couldn't start over and admit that I had been wrong, so my beliefs had to evolve. As I read more, I dropped Wicca for the seemingly more mature witchcraft, which I later traded for animism. No more silly ceremonies, just the basic foundational beliefs. Eventually even that broke down, leaving me where I started: an atheist with an empty life.

That fall I decided to go to church with Melissa. She hadn't pushed me, but I wanted to understand her Christian point of view. I expected something like my family's church with people absent-mindedly reciting prayers. On the contrary, I saw a huge room full of teenagers enthusiastically singing to their God. It frightened me that so many were so deceived. The banners didn't help. They proclaimed some "mission" to Christianize the masses. I wanted to be open to this experience, but I realized I could never be a part of their religion.

The rest of the school year continued without religion or hope. I kept asking my friends my rude questions, although my zeal for disproving them had disappeared. The emptiness of my life began to gnaw at me.

By the end of the school year, new questions were flooding my mind: *What if these Christians really are right? What does that mean for me?* Now I really wanted to know why so many people believed Christianity and why they were even willing to die for it.

A long time after I received the Culture Shock devotional e-mails from Melissa, I decided to subscribe. I hoped to gain a shallow understanding of Christianity so I could argue against it better. But before long I was looking to the devotions for a deeper understanding and something that might fill my empty life. They renamed their devotions TruthWalk, and they became the highlights of my week. I needed to ask my new questions, but I couldn't ask my friends. I was too stubborn to admit that I had been wrong.

I needed to ask someone who didn't know me.
This Rob guy seemed to know a lot, and he certainly
didn't know me.

When I finally decided to ask Rob my questions,
my main goal wasn't to prove him wrong, although I
wasn't ready for him to prove me wrong either.
Fortunately, that was exactly what he set out to do.
He pointed out every crazy idea to which I was cling-
ing. That was painful. All of my already flimsy beliefs
came crashing down together. While tearing my
beliefs to shreds with his gentle answers, he suggested the same beliefs my friends had been sharing
with me all along.

This time I listened.

Rob called these beliefs the "Good News" and
shared with me the need to make a decision. I could
either believe in God or reject Him. My friends had
confronted me with this choice before, but now I
thought more seriously about it because I doubted
God's nonexistence by this time.

I didn't want to believe anything I couldn't
understand, so I asked a lot of questions. All my
inquiries led me to realize that my life was full of my
own immoral actions. It was an overwhelming realiza-
tion. I knew that I could accept God's forgiveness if I
chose to do so. Trust? God? Both concepts sounded

impossible to me. How could I trust Someone I couldn't even see to do something this huge for me? Why would God love me so much to do that, even after all that I had done? And for free? This was incomprehensible, but I wanted to understand.

One cold night, Deb, a lady who works with Rob at Melissa's church, came to my house to take me out for a milk shake. Even though I was a complete stranger to her, she drove thirty minutes to answer my questions. She simplified everything so I could understand. She analogized believing in God's existence to believing in the wind's existence: I can't see the wind, but I can feel its effects. In the same way, I can't see God, but I can feel His effects through the love of those around me.

Even after our discussion, the idea of trusting God was too big and too hard for me to do. Deb told me that I didn't have to make a decision right then. She prayed for me in the middle of the fast food restaurant to have the courage to trust God. That gesture of hers showed me that she cared for me. It made me realize how strong her faith really was.

When I got home, I wanted more than ever to trust God. My mom asked me what I had talked to Deb about, and I told her we talked about good things. Later that night I went to my room and curled up in a little ball on my bed. I didn't know what I was going to do, but I knew I had to do something. I talked to God, who I still wasn't sure existed, and pleaded for something that would assure me that He was there and that I could trust Him. I ran Deb's assurances through my head again and again, hoping that everything would fall together. I finally decided to simply trust God. I opened my heart and became His child.

At that moment, I was more excited than I've ever been in my life. I couldn't contain myself. I left my room and leaped around the house while my family was sleeping. Then I went to the computer and e-mailed everyone to tell them what had just happened.

When I found Wicca, I was elated; however, there is a major difference between Wicca and Christianity. I now have joy, and it has lasted. I no longer have to ask myself, *What is the point of my life?* I have found something real. Becoming a Christian has given me a new outlook on life and more joy than I ever thought possible. Though Christianity was once a culture shock for me, it is now the truth that has changed my life.

REAL QUOTE

Hopefully we can show that we're different from what people expect, and after that we might be able to actually show them what Christianity is truly like: a relationship with God, not just some cultural group that does certain activities, listens to certain music, and disrespects everybody else.

—MATT W., AGE 17

MY PRAYER

Dear Jesus, all I want is the truth, something to believe in that will last. Help me to open my heart and trust in You. Thank You that You are not afraid of hard questions. Thank You that Your truth gives me freedom.

"MY DAD HIT ME LAST NIGHT. IT WASN'T THE FIRST TIME EITHER."

OUR LITTLE FAMILY SECRET

By Shana W., Age 24

Three different high school coaches watched me play my freshman year. Then I heard the big news. A coach from the University of Southern California had shown some interest. I ran home and told my mom and dad. "It looks like I might get to play at college someday," I said.

I waited with anticipation to hear their response. My dad stared at me. "You aren't ever going to be good enough to go to college," he said. "What makes you think you will amount to anything?"

I was angry. Couldn't he see how excited I was? Didn't he understand that I had dreams? "I *am* good enough!" I shouted. "They wouldn't have asked about me if I wasn't." My anger overrode the danger signals thick in the air. "I'm going to be better than this family. I can be better than any of you!"

My dad ripped me out of the chair, and his fists beat down as I tried to get away. My leg got caught, and I watched in horror as my dad aimed and kicked my kneecap with his boot. I screamed as the ligaments tore, and my kneecap twisted.

"Now let's see how good you can be at basketball," he said. He turned and left me alone with my injuries and my broken dreams. Basketball wasn't just something that I was good at; it was my refuge. After-school practices meant I didn't have to go home until late. Games occupied at least part of my nights.

When I went to the doctor, he confirmed what I already knew. My kneecap was pushed out of socket. The bones were chipped at the bottom and top of my knee. My ligaments were torn. I doubted I would ever heal quickly enough to play. The loss of even one season is a huge deal for any athlete, and an injury like this would take at least a year or more to heal.

But it wasn't the injury that plagued me the most. Instead, it was the question I asked for the next couple of years: *Would I really have been good enough to play for Southern California?* I convinced myself that the loss wasn't as huge as it seemed. *I probably wouldn't have been good enough,* I reasoned. At any rate, that was not my first injury, and it wouldn't be my last, as long as I lived in this home.

We called them spankings, but they were beatings. There was the time I didn't get the mail out of the mailbox after school; my arm was broken for that mistake. Once, my father stood on the back steps and aimed a loaded shotgun, counting down as my younger brother fled for his life. My dad pulled the gun to his shoulder and shot at my helpless brother, who stumbled through the woods. We had no clue whether he was all right or not. We could only hope.

I tried to protect my little brothers from my dad. I hid them in the closet or in the woods behind our home whenever my dad was angry. There were times when I woke up and needed to go to school, and my parents were nowhere to be found. They might be on a drinking binge or at an auction. The longest time they were gone was seventeen days. During that time, I sent my brother to school and stayed home with my baby brother. If that was what it took for us to survive, I would do it. I felt as though I had been an adult from the age of ten.

All of my family, except for my dad's parents, lived within ten miles of each other. Our family was close, but it was not a normal closeness. The women in my family had all been abused, from the youngest to the oldest. Among the kids, it wasn't "I was grounded." It was "my leg got broken last weekend." Everybody knew what was going on at each other's house. We all went to the hospital together. There were generations of abuse in the entire family, but it was the only family I knew.

That's why I was shocked when my parents decided we were going to leave California. I ran away three times. I was sixteen, and I didn't want to leave my friends or my family. It didn't matter how much I begged my parents to stay; we eventually moved to be closer to my dad's parents.

At my new home I fell into a pattern. I went to school and came back home. Having lost basketball and being without friends, I began to experiment with alcohol and smoking. I hung out with people that I shouldn't. They weren't really friends, but it was something to do.

Little things continued to set my dad off. We never knew when he would blow up. I hated my dad, and I hated my mom because I didn't understand why she let these things happen to her kids.

One day I was at school, and there were some girls in the lunch line. They were complaining because someone was cutting in line. I asked them for $20 and said I would beat him up. They thought I was joking, but they gave me the $20. I walked up to the guy and beat him up and promptly was suspended from school.

The funny part is that these girls were Christians. One girl called and apologized for the fact that I had been suspended. She said it was wrong for them to offer me money, even in fun. When I went back to school, I saw them from time to time. My lunch hour was changed, and by coincidence so was theirs. They asked me to eat lunch with them, so I did. I listened as they talked about things like God and church and Teens for Christ. I didn't ask them any questions because we weren't really close friends; they were just people to eat lunch with.

I spent a lot of time at my home drinking. One night my family was gone, and I found my dad's 357 magnum. I wrote a note, put one bullet in the gun, and shot it once at my earlobe. Nothing. Then I put it to my throat. The gun wouldn't go off. The phone rang, and I set down the gun. It was one of the girls, and she wanted to know if I wanted to come over. I was drunk, and I didn't have a car, so I said no, but then I was too chicken to pull the trigger anymore.

The girls asked me to go to church with them. It was something to do, so I went. Pam and Ike Jacquez were the youth pastors of the church. My parents didn't care if we were away from home, so I spent a lot of time with my new friends at church and with Pam and Ike.

The summer after my senior year I went to youth camp. My mom had always said that I could never leave home until after I graduated. When camp was over, I moved in with the youth pastors and lived with them for over a year. Because their family was so different from mine, I thought their home was abnormal, but in a really wonderful way. I loved living there. It was peaceful. I always knew that the way I was raised was wrong, but I thought every family went through it. For the first time in my life, I knew the difference.

I had to move back home because my baby brother, who was now ten years old, was getting beaten up. It was hard leaving the security and peace of the Jacquez home, but I had no choice. I needed to protect him.

One day I was walking with a friend from church. I had heard her testimony and wondered if this was someone who might understand. I casually asked her a question about her past. She shared how God had helped her and her family through hard times when she was younger.

I really struggled. *Could I tell someone?* I had kept the secret inside for twenty-one years. There was a time when I called the cops because I feared for my mom or brothers' lives, but every time they came out, it was four people's word against one's.

My parents said I was a liar. My brothers said it was only a spanking. I finally gave up trying to get help and dealt with it the best I could.

I had learned not to let people get close to me. Even in church I moved from seat to seat each week so people wouldn't get close and suspect what was going on.

"How come your knee clicks when you walk?" my friend asked as we walked. I wore a brace, and I didn't think my bad knee was that obvious.

I gave her one of the answers I gave everybody: I fell. I hurt it playing basketball. Whatever—anything but the truth. We walked farther, and I wrestled with telling her the truth.

"I didn't hurt my knee playing basketball," I blurted out, and for the first time I told someone about my family. I didn't expect help, or maybe I did. I don't know. All I know is that once I started to tell it, I told the whole story. It was a relief to finally let someone in on our little family secret.

I left the next week with the church on a trip. Before I left, I wrote my dad a note and told him that I wanted to be healed, to be free of my past. I felt that I had to get beyond what had happened to me. In the note I wrote that I forgave him and that I loved him. I couldn't remember ever telling my dad that I loved him before that day.

When I came back home, it was a Friday night. Before I had left, my baby brother had attended church with me and had accepted Christ into his life. As my dad and I talked about it, I told my dad that he needed to go easier on him. We argued for a few moments, and then my dad opened his arms like he wanted to hug me. I walked into his arms, and he wrapped them around me. Then he hit me in the back of the head and neck, and I fell. As I lay on the floor, he kicked me and pushed me into the cabinets. He kicked me over and over again. As I lay there, I cried out, "Satan, please stop." My dad stopped cold and left the room.

The next day at church my friend approached me and asked me why I was holding my collarbone at an odd angle. I told her, and she asked me to come home with her. I lived with my friend for the next few weeks until I could move out on my own. The church helped me find and move into an apartment.

I continued to go to church. One night, someone sat beside me and asked if they could pray for my knee. The next morning I bent to pick up my brace and realized there wasn't any pain. I jumped, and there was still no pain. I was healed! It amazed me that my Heavenly Father could give me back what my earthly father had taken away.

Today I am married to a youth pastor. I share my story with our teens, but we have also opened up our home to foster kids. Even though I'm in my early twenties, we have asked for young teens who have faced abuse.

Our foster kids think that no one understands. If they challenge me and say, "You have no clue what I have gone through," I share what I faced. They trust me because they know I understand. I tell them that God can take them out of hell—not just a spiritual hell, but also the day-to-day misery that they have faced. I want them to know that someone has confidence in them and that they can be whatever God wants them to be. I promise them that there will never be family secrets in our house.

Some call me a survivor, but I don't dwell in the past. I look at my life as it is now. This is who I am, who I was always meant to be.

REAL QUOTE

If you are being abused, don't wait.
Tell someone. If they don't listen, keep talking
until you find someone who will hear you.
God loves you more than you'll ever know.

—SHANA W., AGE 24

MY PRAYER

Dear Jesus, You know what it is like to be bruised and broken. You know what it is to suffer. I pray that You would help me to tell someone. God, let them really listen. I ask that You protect me. I ask that You help my life to be different than my parents' lives. I will learn from You so that one day my children will not know the things I have suffered. Thank You that I am never truly alone because I have You. I thank You that I will have a future that is full and good and guided by You.

"MY FRIENDS TELL ME THEY THINK I'M AN ADDICT, BUT I DON'T THINK SO. I WAS WONDERING IF YOU COULD TELL ME WHAT THE SYMPTOMS ARE."

NO LIMITS

By Chad L., Age 18
(As told to Debbie Lawson)

I was walking down a dirt road and crying out to God. I said, "If You want me, take me. Use me. I give everything to You. I'm going back on the streets, and I'm either going to become sold out to You or sold out to the drug world."

God heard me that day!

When I was young, I discovered it was easy to gain attention by shocking people. When I was nine years old, I smoked pot with teens. In the sixth grade a teacher found rolling papers and a tiny amount of pot in my wallet.

What do you do with an eleven-year-old who has marijuana? My parents arrived at the police

station, and I was punished with an at-home sen-
tence. At age twelve, I started stealing from the
local grocery store. At thirteen, I was fighting and
spouting off to teachers and coaches. I loved sports
and was pretty good at baseball, basketball, and
football, but I couldn't stand the discipline. I
thought I could accomplish a lot if they would let me
do it my way.

As a high school freshman, I was hanging out
with kids three to four years older than I. I had tried
every drug that I knew of except heroin. I didn't
finish the ninth grade. That next summer I started
partying hard. I was known as the guy who didn't
have any limits. If others were taking one or two
pills, I took four or six. Whatever the limit, I beat it.

One night I overdosed on drugs and alcohol and
slept for three days. Another time, the phone rang,
and my mom ran out the door to find me. I had been
beaten, and when she came to pick me up, I was
covered with blood but was too wasted to feel the
pain or even remember what had happened. This
became my life.

I became quite a thief to support my habits. I
stole from my parents' wallets and took anything they
left lying around to hock for money. My older brother
was disgusted with me. He couldn't keep anything
safe from me. I even traded his shirts and shoes for

cash. I didn't limit my stealing to my family either. Once, I stole jewelry off my neighbor's dresser.

When I was fourteen, I was arrested for drug use. My mom wanted me to go to a rehabilitation facility. I agreed to go because I was miserable. I lived as if I were walking a fine line. I attempted to abide by the probation rules, yet I still got high and lived my own life.

Rehab turned out to be a huge joke. The other teens played their parents and the staff and pretended to be straight, but they were all getting high anyway. I came back home, and within two weeks I was arrested again. It was a long year. I tried to follow the rules but always ended up getting in trouble because I stole, lied, and cheated. Finally I had so many probation violations that I had to go back to court.

While I was in court, my mom told the judge about a program called Teen Challenge. The judge and probation division recommended a state mental hospital for treatment, but my mom pleaded with the judge, and he sided with her and agreed to send me to this place.

When I arrived at Teen Challenge, I quickly decided that my behavior wouldn't get me very far. The first day I challenged the staff, and that afternoon I dug up a tree stump with a single shovel and then filled in the hole. Hands full of calluses quickly changed my attitude.

Very slowly, the love that the staff members were showing me made a difference. I started to believe that the love of Jesus Christ that they professed was real. These people understood where I came from. Many of the staff had abused drugs at one time but were radically changed by God's love. They knew how hardened my heart was and seemed to understand that it might take a long time for me to accept their message or even their love for me.

There were days I wanted to run home, but I knew the judge would either send me to a state hospital or to jail. I made two trips back home for breaks and slipped back into my old drug use each time, but it was different.

It was no longer easy or fun.

That brought me to the place God found me. I was desperate for answers. I decided to give up control of my life. Each day I was hungry for His Word and for righteousness. Instead of craving attention, I began to crave sincerity. I was drawn to people around me who were real in their relationship with God.

I graduated from Teen Challenge in a record eight months. Two months later I traveled to China with a group called Youth with a Mission. I have a soft heart for children and those who are poor. This trip changed my life even more.

When I returned from China, I shared my testimony with a couple of local church youth groups. The teens who knew me before couldn't believe I was the same person. Even my appearance had changed.

I hooked up with Youth with a Mission and joined their training sessions in Denver, Colorado. Now I am traveling across the world on short-term mission trips. In addition to China, I have traveled to Cambodia and Vietnam. Because of my past, I have no problem talking to the people who don't know Jesus about Him no matter where they live or what their situation might be. I know how desperately people need God because I needed Him. I know that the hole in a person's heart grows bigger and bigger until God fills it.

This year I celebrated my eighteenth birthday. If God hadn't listened to the prayer of a desperate teen, I don't know where I would be. As it is, I'm on my way to my destiny. There are no limits to where God can take me.

REAL SCRIPTURE

Seek his will in all you do,
and he will direct your paths.

PROVERBS 3:6 NLT

MY PRAYER

Dear Jesus, I am tired of living like this. I hate the person whom I have become. It is hard for me to understand that You might have mercy, but deep inside of me I believe that You do. Change my heart and my destiny. Forgive me of the choices I have made, and help me as I turn away from my old lifestyle and embrace You. Thank You for hearing me when I cried out to You. Thank You for making me a new person.

SURRENDER

By Jennifer H., Age 19

I want to walk closer
I want to be more than just a casual friend
I don't want to be just another poser
I want to stand firm until the end

There is a deep thirst
For doing what is pure and right
But my past has left me cursed,
Tripping and stumbling through the night

It starts with just a thought
I scramble to fight, pushing it away
Before I know it, I'm caught
My entire mind in disarray

What will it take for me to learn
I can't do anything on my own?
There's only one place I can turn,
And cast my cares upon the throne

I'm giving up my solo fight,
Joining forces with the Creator of the world
Invincible as my will and His power unite
In His love, the darkness no longer unfurls!

When the darkness tries to enter
I cast it to my Savior, and out of my way
My thoughts around Christ I'll center
My mind no longer to wander astray!

Finally, letting everything go
Is not the easiest thing to do
Only complete surrender can show
My God's glory shining through.

"I'M TIRED OF FIGHTING THE SAME OLD BATTLES. SOMETIMES I THINK IT WOULD BE EASIER TO GIVE UP."

TOUGH TIMES

By Samantha Z., Age 21

The first thing to greet me in Reynosa, Mexico, was a spider. "Look before you sit," an adult warned. "Also, look up. Tarantulas can fall from above and give you a good scare." I hate spiders, especially huge hairy spiders.

My best friend and I had decided to travel to Mexico with a group called Youth for Christ. It was my first experience away from home, and I knew no one except for my best friend. We dealt with extreme conditions, and the heat was unbelievable. We were told to drink water all day to avoid dehydration. I was trying, but I'm not much of a water drinker. "Drink, or you could die," the leaders warned, so I sipped water, trying to acquire a taste for it.

I started the week thinking I could do it on my own, but halfway through I found that the combination of the food, extreme heat, and home-sickness was overwhelming. I had worked so hard to convince my parents to allow me to go, and now all I could think about was leaving.

I could not make it on my own. I walked to my tent. I was crying, telling my friend that I couldn't do it. I slipped to my knees, feeling completely humbled by my inadequacy. My friend sat beside me and prayed for me, and an incredible peace came over me. I was able to turn it all over to God in that moment. For the rest of the week, I was able to concentrate on the real reason for being there—sharing the love of Christ with others.

A few months later I was waving good-bye once again. My parents drove the five hours to my school and helped me unload. I watched the taillights of their car as they drove away. It wasn't just the thought of being on my own that was hard; I also had to leave all of my friends.

I had learned my lesson. I couldn't do it on my own. I had to trust God to be with me through the difficult times. The hardest part of leaving was saying good-bye to friends. At home I was on a coed soccer team and was friends with the coach's son. When we both left for college, we promised to keep in contact through e-mail and letters. We talked on the phone often, and eventually our friendship deepened. Over the next three years our friendship grew strong, but my friend changed a lot. He hated school. He wasn't happy with his job, and he changed majors often. It seemed as if he didn't enjoy life anymore. I tried to tell him how much Christ loved him and that God had a plan for his life. He told me that he wanted to be a Christian but that he had to straighten out his life first. He wanted to be a good person. Only then would he become a Christian.

I could never seem to get him to understand that God wanted him just the way he was or that God loved him for who he was. I could not convince him that he could not change on his own. I wanted him to understand that God could be with him through the hard times, but he didn't get it.

He started talking to a counselor at school, and his family and I both thought that he was doing better. He was happy again, or at least he seemed to be. He was still confused about life and what he was going to do, but he had dreams for the first time in a long time.

One summer day I was baby-sitting. I was helping the girls get into their swimsuits when a knock came at the door. My mom and pastor's wife stood outside. My mom's face was tear streaked. "What, Mom?" I asked. "What's going on?"

My mom wrapped her arms around me. "Matt is dead," she said. "He's gone, sweetheart." Just like that, one minute my friend is smiling and laughing with me, and the next I was alone. My friend had decided that he couldn't go on and had taken his own life.

I called someone to watch the girls, and I left with my mom. She took me to Matt's parents' house. They opened their arms to me, understanding how much I cared for my friend, and we all wept together.

Somehow God gave me the strength to go on with my own life. I can never change my friend's decision, but I can learn from it. I value my friends more now. I tell them how much I love them and what they mean to me. I can see the value of life and how quickly everything can change. Through the healing process, I have also discovered that God can use the hard times in my life to strengthen me in my walk with Him. Tough times build my faith and teach me to trust in Him.

Attending Matt's funeral was difficult. I asked a friend to go with me. She drove the six hours to my home and attended the funeral. I later found out that she, too, was suicidal, but Matt's funeral helped her to see the impact that suicide can have on those left behind. She and a teacher talked about it during the six-hour drive back to her home.

Matt didn't know how much he was loved and how many people will miss him. I wish that he could have looked past that one moment when life seemed too hard to go on. I wish he were still here.

I won't forget the memory of my friend. I plan to be a teacher, and I want to be a light to the students in my class. I hope to help them realize that suicide is not an option. If they lose a friend or loved one to suicide, I will understand what they are experiencing.

I have to admit that I still struggle with the loss of my friend. Suicide is a hard thing to handle, and I knew right from the start to go to Christ. I have to have faith to make it through my grief.

I now have more of a desire to reach the lost and tell them how much God loves them. If you are facing suicidal thoughts and feel so down about life that you don't think you can go on, let me tell you how much Christ loves you. Life is never so bad that it needs to end because you are not alone. There is a better way. God can and will help you make it through the hard times.

REAL SCRIPTURE

The Lord is close to the brokenhearted;
he rescues those who are crushed in spirit.

—PSALM 34:18 NLT

MY PRAYER

Dear Jesus, there are so many hurting people in this world. All the things that society offers us are not enough. I know that I cannot change my friend's heart, but help me to share the message that You can. Thank You that You love my friend who is struggling. Help me to know the right words to say, and prepare my friend's heart to receive the message that You care.

THE CROSS

By Lawrana M., Age 14

The cross that hangs from my neck
    is a symbol of who I am

What I hold close to my heart
    some people will never understand

He died for them, too,
    not just for me

If they knew someone died
    on Calvary,

Would they wear this cross
    like me?

Or is this a secret that everyone knows
    and chooses not to believe

Not comprehending it comes with love
    and forgiveness for eternity

*"YOU SAY THAT GOD IS LIKE A FATHER.
I GUESS YOU'VE NEVER MET MY DAD."*

CALIFORNIA DREAMING

By Mike H., Age 24

When I was growing up, I watched television a lot. I sat transfixed as the cartoon superheroes fought evil. The imaginary heroes gave me something powerful to believe in. In reality, I needed someone to look up to because my father didn't make a very good hero.

Our home was a house of drug addicts, drunkards, and adultery. Once when my baby sister was three years old, she walked around the living room with a small bag of cocaine. Someone had left it on the floor from a party the night before. My other sister knew what it was and knocked it out of her hand.

My dad cheated on my mom constantly, even having a baby with someone we knew. It tore up our family. My mom and dad stayed together through the affairs until I was seventeen years old.

I never loved my dad, but I never hated him either. I did, however, fear him. I never knew when he would transform. His happy smile would suddenly erupt into a teeth gnashing, temper tantrum of which I was the target. My dad punished me almost every day for little things, like falling behind in my schoolwork or not paying attention when he talked. It made me very angry. A man whose own sins seemed to overshadow my childish mistakes by miles inflicted deep bruises that marked my lower back all the way down to my thighs.

I knew a little bit about God. I knew that He might let me go to Heaven if I was good enough, but I also knew that I was heading down my dad's path. My family said that when they saw me, they saw him. Knowing that, I ruled out any chance that God was going to let me into Heaven. Just in case, I asked God to forgive me every night before I went to bed in the hope that if I died, I would be allowed in Heaven. But the moment I woke up, I knew I was going to choose to impress my friends instead of God.

I had a lot of friends. Though I was white and they were Hispanic, they treated me like a brother. We all hung out in the streets. I was one of the few white kids who hung out in that particular area. I had heard about racism, but in my part of the world, Bakersfield, California, we flocked together on the streets. We were family. I learned loyalty, respect, and freedom. My street family meant independence from my parents, sisters, and my home life.

Though I had a new "family," I still felt alone. I was depressed, sad, angry, and in fear of my future. I never joined a gang. I could have easily, but my friends wanted to steal, drink, get high, or die for the wrong reasons or even the wrong colors. I did learn a few lessons from my dad. Watching him and his friends made me stay away from drugs and drinking. I lived a strange life. I didn't steal or drink or join a gang, but I ran with those who did. I didn't fit in anywhere.

Sleep became my hideout. It wasn't unusual for me to nap three or four hours every afternoon after school. I stayed in bed for hours at a time on weekends. Soon sleeping became just as dangerous for me as staying awake. I had dreams that wouldn't go away. I woke up with sweat drenching my clothes, only to realize that it was a dream. But as soon as I closed my eyes, I slipped back into the frame of the same dream that I had left only moments before.

One dream in particular haunted me. I was in a dark room, down on my knees, surrounded by people. The strangers wore dark clothing and prayed. As the gentle sound of their voices floated in my dream, I moved my lips, talking to God, asking for forgiveness as I always did. All of a sudden the ground opened up beneath me like a cave. The darkness started to swallow me and pull me into its grasp.

The people reached out, grabbed me, and then set me down on firm ground. I stared into their faces, but I didn't recognize them—except for one person, my grandma.

When I woke up, I was exhausted and confused. I decided I needed to stop sleeping so much.

The strange thing is I was running toward God in my dreams, but in real life I was walking in an entirely different direction. I went to church on occasion. I was even baptized, but it didn't mean anything to me. A couple of days after my baptism, I went right back to my old lifestyle, and I was stuck right back in depression.

A year later, my dad finally ran off with someone else. Every member of our family of five now had to fend for his or her self. My sisters moved in with my dad and his girlfriend. My mom moved in with her mother. I wondered if anyone was worried where I was supposed to go. But after all, I was seventeen years old, and I had a smart mouth. Maybe they didn't want to hear what I had to say. Maybe they didn't want me around, and leaving me behind was their way of giving me the message.

After a few days of wandering from place to place, my grandma asked if I wanted to stay with her. She invited me to church, but I turned her down. She never pressured me but told me she was concerned because of my anger, depression, and the violent tantrums that I threw. Grandma introduced me to the books of Psalms and Proverbs. My life was so messed up that King David started to make sense, especially his struggles. He had looked for peace, and I was on the same search. I found it in my grandma's house. There, my insides stilled, and my rage went away. Grandma said that God lived in her house and that made it our sanctuary.

Grandma's pastor came by one day and asked if I wanted to play basketball in the park. I started trash talking while we played. He challenged me, saying that if he beat me one-on-one, I had to come to church on Sunday. I said it was "all good" and if he lost, he had to buy me a soft drink. I figured I'd let him down easy.

After just a few minutes, the score was 10-2 in my favor. I gave him a hard time, telling him what flavor soft drink he should buy. All of a sudden the guy dropped to his knees on the concrete. He looked up at the sky and started praying, saying, "Lord, help me to win this game for Your glory."

I interrupted him, saying, "You can pray all you want. All I have to do is 'sco-one-mo,' and you're beat." He stood up and smiled and then proceeded to beat me 11-10.

I was tripping. God had never answered my prayers like that. I was there on Sunday before the doors opened, and I waited for him on the front steps. He saw me waiting. He sat beside me and gave me a big hug. He called me "Brother Mikey."

I talked to him, telling him that it seemed as if God were chasing me, and I asked him what I should do.

"Stop running, Mikey," he said.

I did. I was transformed from wrecked goods to a brand-new child of God. I wanted a fresh start. I wanted to move away from all of the people and things that once pulled at me. One night I asked God to help me move away from California. A few days later, my mom and two sisters decided to move to another state, and I went with them.

I wanted to find a church right away. I walked for miles around the new city. I stopped at one large church. A man in a suit stopped me as I walked in. "What do you need?" he asked.

God, I thought.

The man held out his hand and shook mine; then he pulled out a handkerchief as he walked away and wiped his hands. I quickly walked out the door and back into the night. *Looks like I'm not going to find Him here,* I thought.

There was another church not far away. The parking lot was full. The steeple rose in the sky, inviting me to try again. I walked in, and someone came up immediately and shook my hand. Another person showed me the way to the youth group. There, a woman approached me. She looked famil-iar, but I knew that I had never met her. She wrapped her arm around my shoulder and introduced me to several people. I looked different from anyone else in the room with my shaved head and big clothes, but I still felt right at home.

Now I had a new church home with people who cared about me. Later that night when I laid down to sleep, the face of the woman haunted me. *Why did she look so familiar?* I wondered. Then it hit me hard. The woman who had introduced me to others in the group was one of the people in my dream. I thanked God! I realized that He had brought me to a place where people would help me find the strength I needed to live for Him.

Today, five years later, I'm in a Christian rap group called Real Eyes. We practice, write songs at night after work, and rap for youth groups. We hope to cut a CD soon.

I have worked out things with my dad. My depression is gone. My anger is only a memory. I'm not bitter anymore. Forgiveness is my new way of life. I've forgiven myself. I've forgiven my dad, and we are closer than we've ever been. Where there was pain and anger, there is now laughter and real joy. I have a wife and a son named Isaac. I'm determined to be a good father to my son and a good husband to Becky.

In a sense I am still running, but this time I'm headed in the right direction. Instead of my nightmares chasing after me, I'm running after the dreams that God had for me all along.

REAL QUOTE

Sometimes I feel too small and insignificant to be a part of God's plan. But then I see that throughout history God has used the small and insignificant people of this world to carry out His plans. He has taken people whose lives were full of problems and given them the ability to rise above them. He has changed the world through their lives! God can meet me where I am and use me to change my world.

—ERIN P., AGE 17

(Excerpted with permission from *Meditation Warriors Devotions*)

MY PRAYER

Abba Father. That's what Your Word says You are to me—Daddy God. Thank You for being my Abba Father. Thank You for teaching me to be Your child. Help me to walk with You, to learn Your ways, and to be the person You always knew I could be.

DIVINE INSOMNIA, THE RAP

By Mike H.

One night I had a dream
 that I was down on my knees

Surrounded by people
 who were praying for me

They were calling Jesus' name
 and had Bibles in their hands

Praying some kind of words
 I couldn't understand

They prayed so hard,
 they had tears in their eyes

My grandma was the only one
 I could recognize

I could tell by their faces
 that something was going on

Then I looked to the ground,
 and the floor was gone

I started to fall,
 but those people reached down,

Lifted me up,
 and put me back on solid ground

I stared at the faces
   of the people I had never met

But little did I know
   they weren't my church family yet

God woke up people
   to pray for my troubled soul

'Cause I was lost in deep night
   and sin had taken its toll

I let God have control,
   and I'm not afraid anymore

'Cause I'm surrounded by God's people,
   those I met once before

"I'VE GOT A LONG TIME TO LIVE. TAKE YOUR PREACHING SOMEWHERE ELSE. IT'S TIME TO PARTY."

TIME RAN OUT

By Aaron A., Age 19

The guy handed me a joint as I drove down the road. I held it in my fingers, unsure of what to do with it. "It's to pay you back for the ride," he said. I dropped him off and went to a friend's house, showing him what the guy had given me. "What do I do with this?" I asked.

My friend laughed. "It's only a joint. It's not a big deal. Smoke it." That day I experienced my first high. From that time on I started smoking weed. It wasn't hard to find friends who like to get high, and before long I was getting high every day.

Three years later I was still smoking weed, and then a friend gave me crank. I stayed up all night and hated the way it made me feel. I decided that crank wasn't for me. I had a friend who had a lot of money, and he was willing to buy drugs for his friends. He was the one who introduced me to cocaine, and since I didn't have to pay for it, I stayed high most of the time.

Most of the members of my family are Christians, and my uncle is a minister. During this time in my life, my grandma prayed for me all of the time, knowing I was into things that had nothing to do with God. I was torn because I knew what was right and I had no doubt that what I was doing was wrong.

The hardest part for me was that I had experienced God, and I missed my relationship with Him. I began to hate my life as it was. I still liked the way cocaine made me feel, but I didn't like the physical part of doing drugs, pushing them up my nose. Every time I did it, I hated it, and I had God on my mind the whole time. I wished and prayed that I could stop, but I couldn't, so I learned to block out those feelings.

After I graduated from high school, I moved into an apartment. Now that I was alone, I was really depressed and down on myself, but I reasoned that I had plenty of time to change. After all, I was only eighteen years old.

One night I partied with a group of people. We played games and snorted cocaine. I had been high for most of the day. A guy I vaguely knew joined the party. His reputation was that he had been into drugs for a long time. He wasn't standing far from me, and I saw him draw up and start shaking. His body shook violently, and then he dropped to the floor, his whole body in convulsions. Somebody shouted that the guy had stopped breathing. We jumped up from the sofa, and someone resuscitated him.

Someone could have died right in front of me. Someone young. Someone not very different from me.

I went home that night, and I knelt on the floor of my apartment and gave my life back to God. I asked Him for another chance. I knew that it didn't matter if I was young. I was playing with my life, and I wasn't God.

One week later I heard from a friend named Mike. He said he was tired of doing drugs and planned to go to rehab. He wanted to come stay the night with me and then check himself in the next day. I was at work the day he was supposed to come. When I arrived home, I saw my sister's car in front of the apartment. She wasn't supposed to be off work, and I wondered why she was there.

When I walked in, she was crying. "Mike's dead," she said. She paused; her voice was barely a whisper. "Aaron, Mike's not the only one who died."

Then she shared the rest of the gruesome story. Something went wrong and I guess we'll never know what. One of my friends shot Mike, and then he killed another close friend. After that, he killed himself with a lethal drug overdose. They found the two bodies of my friends in a house. Later they found our third friend, the one who had pulled the trigger, in a still-running pickup truck. His body was warm, but it was far too late to save him.

Six best friends. Each of us had been insepara-ble since grade school. Half of our group was gone in seconds, divided by two homicides and a suicide. After the funerals, our town gathered at the high school gymnasium. My friend Tony and I spoke. We shared the mistakes that we had made over the past three years.

Saying good-bye to three friends, all under the age of nineteen years, was the hardest thing I've ever faced. Today I tell teenagers that we don't always have forever. We only have today. I will live day by day because that's all I'm promised, but from now on I'll find my highs in serving God.

REAL QUOTE

Just be who God wants you to be.

—JACOB P., AGE 17

MY PRAYER

Dear Jesus, I've taken for granted the things You've given me—my family, my church, Your love for me. Inside, where no one else can see, You know that I long to love You as my Savior, but I don't know how anymore. I hate "religion," but I would do anything to have a real day-to-day relationship with You. Help me to understand that Your grace is a free gift and all I have to do is receive it. I am reaching out for You today.

FOREVER

By Jimmy G., Age 16

When I was ten,
I was born again,
Held and wrapped up tight
In my Daddy's arms.

Apart from Him,
I was nothing,
But now He lives in my heart.

Now I grow in faith,
And I live by grace,
Was blind but now I see.

Chorus
Gonna live forever,
I'm gonna live forever,
Gonna live forever,
Up in Heaven where my Daddy lives.

Music (two riffs)
It's a Friday night,
I'm feeling just right;
I'm about to go
About to go
To the club.

Then there it came
A voice in my head
Remember what your Daddy said.

He knows the plans for me
A hope and future
To prosper and not to harm.

Gonna live forever,
I'm gonna live forever,
Gonna live forever,
Up in Heaven where my Daddy lives.

(music intermission, then drums change into a rap beat)

Rap
Jesus Christ, Lord of my life,
Takes away my pain and strife
Died on the cross for all our sins
Rose three days later to prove He was Him.

Now take the chance while you can;
Trade your life for His master plan.
Grab a ball, get in the game,
Be among those who seek His name.

Then you can live forever,
You can live forever,
And then you can live forever
Up in Heaven where your Daddy lives.

"FIRST OF ALL, TO BE A 'TRUE CHRISTIAN,' IT ISN'T NECESSARY TO FOLLOW EVERY BIBLICAL COMMANDMENT. THERE IS NO ABSOLUTE TRUTH ON EVERY ISSUE, AT LEAST NOT IN TODAY'S MODERN WORLD."

ABSOLUTE FREEDOM

By Tommy R., Age 24

When I was ten years old, I sat in a warm bathtub and sawed on my wrist with a razor blade, crying out, "Lord, please let me die. It hurts too bad!" I also prayed that the blood would stay in the bathtub and not drip on the carpet. I didn't want my mother to have to clean up the mess.

The suicide attempt wasn't successful, and I learned then that life didn't begin at my will and wouldn't end by it either.

My mom worked shift work at a factory, and my cousins, aunts, and uncles watched over my brother and me while she worked. Sometimes we stayed at our house, and at other times we went to the homes of our aunts and slept. It was like one big sleepover, but it wasn't always fun. There was one individual who made the situation a nightmare. He molested me. By the age of ten, all I knew was that I wanted the unspeakable things that were happening to stop.

By the time I turned sixteen, I was into alcohol and drugs. It was then that the feeling that I didn't understand when I was younger began to have a name attached to it. In high school I experimented with new drugs, new beliefs, and new friends, and I slowly investigated those feelings that went with the new name that I could never say myself. I was scared to admit that I was a homosexual. Every time that I heard someone in my family speak about gay people, it was not in a nice way. I remember the first time I said it out loud: "I think I'm gay."

It was easier than I thought.

I was not a stereotypical homosexual; most aren't. I was an average American guy who was into dating, partying, hanging out—what every other eighteen-year-old I knew was doing.

I wasn't perfect by any means. I used drugs and alcohol a lot, and sometimes I was rebellious with my mom. But I was also a good student who attended church, and I was considered to be a good kid.

I was terrified that my family would discover my secret. I was convinced that they would hate me and reject me even more than I already felt they did. But at the same time, having to keep my life a secret made me angry. *Why couldn't they accept me for the person that I was?* I wondered. *Why couldn't they let me be who I was created to be?* Now more than ever I was convinced that this was a fact.

I continued with my newfound life of freedom. My whole attitude and personality changed as I accepted my new self and grew more confident that this was my path in life. This was my destiny! I'm not sure if my straight friends had any idea, but as time went on, I wondered whether or not most of them were feeling the same thing. There were situations and comments that led me to believe that quite a few of them did. This just added to what I already knew to be true: These feelings weren't bad. In fact, they were normal, natural.

One weekend, two friends and I woke up on a Saturday morning with one thing on our minds, continuing the party from the night before. As I sat in the living room chair, one of my friends removed his dad's .38-caliber pistol from his parents' closet. He showed us how to play Russian roulette. "You take all the bullets out but one, and you spin it like this," he said, demonstrating as he went along. "Then you

put the gun to your head, and you pull the trigger.
It's that simple."

I decided I would rather have a soda than play a
stupid game. I turned to my right to walk into the
kitchen and saw a flash that surprised and blinded
me. The sound of gunfire rang through my head.
After the initial shock, I turned back to my friends.

They had astounded looks on their faces, eyes
larger than hubcaps, chins that dug into the orange
and brown carpet. I remember my friend asking if I
was shot. I thought, *What a stupid question; you
have the gun.* Then I felt a warm sensation running
from my chest to my legs. Blood was staining my
shirt and running all the way to my knees. I felt
around, sick when I realized that my side and part of
my back were also covered in blood.

The EMTs hoisted me into the ambulance. My
friend was in the background, apologizing over and
over. I looked down and saw a package stuck in a
compartment, and it read "bodybag." I walked out
of the hospital six hours later with a hole in my
chest, a great story, and the idea that I was just
plain lucky. After a few sore weeks, I was back to the
life that was mine. It was a life that was becoming
easier to live with each passing day.

Then came college. I was excited. There were more people in one dorm building than there were residents in my hometown. It only took about twenty-four hours to get hooked up with the party crowd. People were very open about their sexuality—gay or straight.

Over the next few months, I watched the homosexuals on campus who lived an openly gay lifestyle. I looked for the well-adjusted and self-accepting whole people that I dreamed they would be. But although they lived in "freedom," there was definitely something missing. This caused me to question myself, *Is this who I am? Is this what I want for my life?*

I wondered if a relationship could be a reality for me. Perhaps that would fix everything. I met several people, but most wanted a purely physical relationship, and I wanted more than that.

The summer break after my twenty-first birthday, I worked at a hospital in a city not far from my hometown. I met people at the most critical moments in their lives. I held the hand of an infant new to the world and comforted those who were dying. I realized very quickly that there is more to this thing called life.

During this time, a co-worker befriended me. She wasn't afraid to express her beliefs. I admired that. She wasn't rude about her personal convictions and was very respectful of others and their way of seeing things, even when they put her down. She was not ashamed to share that Jesus Christ was the center of her life.

At first I didn't want to listen. After all, He had not cared for me as far back as I could remember. She didn't pressure. She just gently reassured me and reminded me that there was Someone who loved me.

As the summer passed, I began to pray. I talked honestly with my friend about my past. She added new insights to the things that I had experienced, but she didn't know my current lifestyle, so I held back. I knew that Christians were quick to say they loved you—until they uncovered something about you that they didn't know how to handle.

My friend invited me to a drama at her church. I turned her down. She then told me about a ministry at her church for people in college, and I decided to go. I was desperate. I prayed, "God, either show me that You are real and love me, or when I get home, I'm going to stick a gun in my mouth and blow my brains out. Amen."

I arrived at seven o'clock, leaving no time for the religious to target me. The pastor spoke to me. He seemed nice, but I wondered if it was a preacher façade. I made it through the service. It was church as usual, no resounding, celestial voice answering my prayers.

As soon as the dismissal was given, I almost ran to the door. I heard a voice behind me call my name, and I turned just in time to see the face of the pastor. He wrapped his arms around my shoulders and said, "I have to tell you something that God spoke into my heart when I saw you." He held me tightly and wouldn't let me go. "He loves you. He said for me to tell you that He loves you, He loves you, He loves you." Something on the inside of me broke. This man didn't know me, but God evidently did. I don't know if anyone else noticed the miracle that happened in the doorway, but a very lost child—a modern-day prodigal son—was running straight into the arms of a loving Father.

I sobbed all the way home. I realized that I had been foolish and that I had hurt for far longer than I needed. I cried because I had turned my back on God. I realized that all the time and in all those places, God was there.

He made me, and He could repair the damage in my soul.

Now that you know a little bit about who I was, let me tell you who I have become. Through the Lord Jesus Christ, I am free. I have found that there *is* absolute truth. It is where it has always been; it is in Christ. My mission in life is restored.

When I preach to others, I tell people who think there is no way out of the pain; the rejection; and the loneliness of alcohol, drugs, and even homosexuality that they can find hope. I have found acceptance. However, it is not through the lie that I believed before—that I am supposed to live a life contrary to the plan God has for me. For me that was alcohol, drugs, and homosexuality. When God brought me into existence, those were not the words that He spoke over my life; He had greater plans than that for me.

I know. I was there, but now I am discovering God's will as I live in His absolute freedom.

REAL SCRIPTURE

"I know the plans I have for you," says the LORD.
"They are plans for good and not for disaster,
to give you a future and a hope."

—JEREMIAH 29:11 NLT

MY PRAYER

Dear Jesus, everyone around me tells me that the life I have chosen is my destiny, but all I've found in this lifestyle is empty promises. I struggle with those people in the church who offer condemnation without answers. Many times, I'm not sure where to turn for help, so I will turn to You. Lord, I dare to believe that You have the ability to change my heart. Renew my mind with Your presence and Your purpose. I'm Yours. Thank You for being mine.

"I HEAR CHRISTIANS TALK ABOUT SEXUAL INTERCOURSE BEFORE MARRIAGE AS BEING WRONG, BUT THEY NEVER TALK ABOUT OTHER SEXUAL STUFF. HOW DO YOU DEFINE SEX?"

OUT OF THE BOX

By Lacynda B., Age 19

When I was seven and attended camp for the first time, I knelt at an altar and asked Christ to be the Lord of my life. This came as no surprise to anyone. My parents were the leaders of the camp. It was just the way it was supposed to be. Mom and Dad were Christians, and now I was too. Living as a Christian seemed more of a hassle than a desire as I grew older. I put up a front at church. I had to pretend I was perfect when I really wasn't, and I hated it. Slowly my heart turned away from God.

When I was thirteen years old, a man who was a friend from church committed suicide. I realized that people who said they were Christians could actually lie about it and live totally non-Christian lives. Worse, I realized that I was doing it too. I didn't want to be a liar, so I turned my back on God.

I was intrigued by the New Age cult. Although I never dove into it, I dabbled with it a great deal. I knew that my parents would freak if they ever found out and that my church would, too, so I didn't tell anyone. I just wanted to get away from God.

When I was fourteen, I met an awesome guy. He said he was a Christian. He went to church and was even involved in the Bible Club at my school. He invited me to the Bible Club and encouraged me to participate more in my church. *Wow, maybe being a Christian isn't such a bad deal,* I thought. We started dating the night we met. I thought it was great to finally meet a Christian who was just like everyone else.

It didn't take long for his "Christian" mask to fade. First it was just stronger, more passionate kisses after school. Then it was longer times in the dark where no one could see us together. I thought it was all exciting and daring until I realized one day that he was going a little too far. I told him to stop.

Two days later I found him with his arms around another girl. The next afternoon he told me we weren't dating anymore.

We never went as far as sex; I wouldn't do that because I knew the consequences. I didn't want a baby. However, we went as far as we could without reaching that point. No one told me what would happen when we broke up. No one told me that I had given a part of myself away with those kisses and times together in the shadows. No one told me how it would feel the next day to see someone else in his arms and know that I used to be that someone. No one told me about the shame that I would have to live with.

I didn't want to date after that. If this is how I would feel every time I went out with someone and then broke up, then I didn't want any part of it. I couldn't look at myself in the mirror anymore.

I didn't want friends around. What did they see in me? Why were they looking at me like that? Surely they were talking about me. Why else would they be whispering?

I isolated myself from my friends, my family, and especially guys. I knew what they wanted, and it wasn't friendship. I knew that every guy was alike and that they all wanted the same thing.

When I was fifteen, I went to camp. I had discovered a secret: the more hateful I was to people, the easier it was to make them leave me alone. No

one wanted to be around me at camp, and that's
how I wanted it. But on the inside I hurt so bad that I
felt like I was dying. Something was missing in my
life, something important. Everything at camp
seemed so dead, just like me.

One night I sat in a camp service. "Everyone
lives in a box," the speaker said. "We can either
choose to leave the windows of the box open so that
people can come in and our emotions can go out, or
we can choose to close up the windows and keep
everyone on the outside from coming in. This effec-
tively keeps all your emotions locked deep inside.
Some people try to lock God out in the same way."

In that moment I realized I was hiding from
God. I had turned my back on Him. I had locked up
everything inside of me, and I let no one touch me. I
walked to the front of the room and tried to stand at
the altar, but I fell to my knees and wept. It felt so
good to be able to cry again. My hardened heart
broke before God. It was like two strong arms
enveloped me, and I heard the words "I love you"
deep inside of me. I knew it was God speaking to me.

I sat at the altar for two hours, but when I got
up I was a new person. God took my cold, hardened
heart and broke it and put it back together. He took
the shame away and in return gave me a love for Him.

One of my favorite scriptures is 2 Corinthians 5:17. It reads that those who become Christians become new persons. "They are not the same anymore, for the old life is gone. A new life has begun!" (NLT). That's me. My life began when I turned it over to Him.

Today I am still completely changed. I have sincerely followed Christ for almost five years. God gave me wonderful friends and taught me that not all guys are hormone-crazed jerks. I dated a guy for almost two years, and he taught me that love is more than just physical attraction. It's something much deeper.

When you open your heart, no other love can compare with that of Jesus Christ.

REAL SCRIPTURE

Don't let anyone look down on you because you are young, but set an example for the believers in speech, in life, in love, in faith and in purity.

—1 TIMOTHY 4:12 NIV

MY PRAYER

Dear Jesus, You will never crush my heart. You will never leave me standing alone with lies and deceit as my only companions. Thank You for loving me as Your child. Thank You for renewed purity that comes only through Your healing touch. Lord, help me to see myself in the mirror of Your love and to accept nothing less than Your best.

IF YOU REALLY LOVE ME

By Celine Marie F. M., Age 13

If you really love me,
You'll treasure me like a jewel.
I'll know you're not playing around,
I'll know you're not a fool.

If you really love me,
You'll wait for our wedding day.
You'll keep yourself pure,
Not throw yourself away.

Your eyes will not search
For things they should not see.
You'll keep your thoughts moral,
And save yourself for me.

You'll talk to my parents,
And keep your promise true.
You'll love me for me,
And I, you for you.

When you take me out,
Your hands won't cross the line.
I'll know that I'm yours,
And you'll know that you're mine.

"ALL I WANT IS A NORMAL LIFE LIKE EVERYBODY ELSE. IT SEEMS AS IF GOD HAS FAVORITES."

LIVING PROOF

By Brandon G., Age 16

My life started out normal. I had a good home. My mom was really there for me, but everything changed when my parents divorced. My mom had to work hard to take care of us. Later, she remarried, and for a while things were better, but then my family started struggling again. For some reason, we were always low on money.

When I was twelve years old, my step-brothers came to live with us. They were literally dropped off on the front porch. Money for food was tight. My step-dad was trying to take care of all of us, but it steadily got worse, and we were forced to take my step-brothers back to Texas. When we got back home, we realized that things were much worse than we thought. My step-dad was picked up by the police and sent to jail. We discovered that he had been dealing drugs and was addicted. In fact, he had been using drugs for a long time; we just hadn't realized it. Now everything started to make sense.

The police released him after a couple of days, but he went right back to using. This time is was no longer a secret. This started a cycle. My step-dad would be arrested and then released. Each time he went back to using. My step-dad's drug use had a tight hold on him, but worse, it had a grip on us. We couldn't afford rent, so my mom, my little sister, and I moved to another city to live with my aunt. Money was still tight because now there were two families to feed. My mom was a nurse and worked a lot of hours to help support us. The only time I got to see her was after work late at night. My step-dad was on the run from the police, so he only came by after dark.

I started hanging out with the wrong crowd. I wasn't looking for trouble; I just wanted something to do. I didn't want to go home because it wasn't the greatest place to be since my family was never there. I started hanging out with skaters, and some of them used drugs. At thirteen years old, I started partying and drinking with them.

Living with my aunt brought new trouble. One night I was at a party with my aunt's friends. I met this man who was about thirty-five years old. He was a drug dealer and gave me free drugs and alcohol, anything that I wanted. I didn't trust him, and I told him that, but he just laughed and gave me more drugs and alcohol. By the end of the night, I was so drunk I couldn't even walk. I felt this man touching me in the wrong way, and I told him to back off, but he wouldn't stop. He continued to touch me against my will. I screamed at him to get away from me. A friend heard me and knocked the guy off of me and pushed him down to the ground. I staggered away.

My mom found out, and we moved again. But things weren't much different at our new location. I was still messing with drugs and having sex. My step-dad was still using drugs. Mom was still trying to hold all of us together. Then I found out the worst news yet: My mom had Hepatitis C. For the first time, the one person who had always been strong was having to battle just to stay healthy.

I decided I needed to be a man. My mom was pregnant and sick. My little sister was only four years old. It was up to me to protect them. I turned fourteen, and I bought a gun. I gave all the money I had to buy a 9 mm pistol.

The police caught up with my step-dad. They stormed into our home and slammed us all against the wall, screaming and shouting. The whole block watched as they streamed into our house. A cop wrestled my pregnant mom to the floor. I held my sister, Laney, in my arms, and they slammed us out of the way. I fell with her, and I tried to protect her by wrapping my body around her. Several cops jumped my step-dad as we watched. My mom was screaming that she was pregnant, and the policeman finally let her go. They handcuffed my step-dad, and then a policeman told my mom that she had five minutes to get rid of everything in the house.

My step-dad had drugs everywhere, so she and I frantically tried to get rid of everything. The policeman said that they would be back and our house better be clean. If it wasn't, Mom would go to jail, and Laney and I would go to the state.

Things were now tighter than ever at our home. My mom was very sick now, and my step-dad was in jail. It was so hard to make ends meet, to buy food, and to pay the rent. I decided that I was the tough kid and that I would help out, so I collected money that people owed my step-dad.

One day a man came by our house. I was leery of strangers, but he introduced himself. His name was Tim Wallace. He was part of a street ministry for a nearby church. He talked to my mom about the possibility of us going to church. He came by another evening after work, and I went with him to the service. I wasn't too interested in what was going on that night. It was like a different world—interesting, but it didn't seem to have anything to do with me.

For two months, I avoided Tim. He would stop by on occasion. One day I decided to give church another try. This time I watched the people in the youth group. They all seemed happy, but again they didn't understand my world. When people asked me if I wanted to be saved, I said no.

I waited four or five months, checking everything out. Then one night I realized that I didn't want to wait anymore. I wanted to experience what I had seen happen in other people's lives. I wanted to know if I could have what Tim had. I left that night with a desire to be different. I still smoked, and I was still drinking, but I quit taking drugs. The more I grew in my faith, the more I was able to change. The biggest change was that I was able to forgive the people who had hurt me. Sometimes it's hard to forgive when the bad things that happen to you aren't your fault, but God gave me the grace to do it anyway. It wasn't an overnight change. I was still fighting. I was still acting tough. I thought I had to do that to survive. Most people probably thought that I was still an unbeliever, but I wanted to know God, and something new had definitely begun in my life.

By now, I was fifteen years old, and I wanted more from God. I realized that I had a drinking problem, and though I wasn't sure if God could help me with it, I was willing to give it to Him.

I became very involved in my youth group. I joined the activities, and I went places with them. I actually had fun. It surprised me that I could have more fun with these people when I was sober than I could with my old friends at a party. There were a couple of people who helped me as I tried to change. Jason Rose was three years older than me and was the pastor's son. He called every day after school, asking me how I did that day and letting me know that he was praying for me. Oftentimes, he came by my house, picked me up, and took me out to eat. He also drove me to the youth pastor's house, and we would hang out there. It was awesome.

Slowly, I let go of the drinking as my faith in God grew stronger. Though I was changing, things were the same at home. We were once again forced to leave. Mom was still sick, and now she had a baby to take care of in addition to Laney and me. We moved to another state to live with some friends and to get away from the old neighborhood where we lived.

I was praying for my mom, and I realized that she looked better than she had in a long time. She had been really thin for a long time, and she was finally gaining weight. The doctors in Louisiana gave us great news. They said that she was in remission. That was the best news we had received in a long time! Things were looking up.

I started looking for a church and met a couple of Christian guys right away. One of them was a pastor of a small church. When I went to his church on Sundays and Wednesdays, I wrote notes from the sermon and went home and read them to my mom. She listened to me with tears in her eyes, and I could see that she loved hearing them and that she loved watching me grow in my faith.

Christ was growing inside of me. My old lifestyle held no part of me anymore. We stayed in Louisiana for four months, and then we moved back to be close to my step-dad who was still in prison. Mom got a job, and we were getting by.

My step-dad was up for parole in a few months. I wasn't sure how I felt about our family getting back together. Things were going better for us than they had in a long time. I worried about how my step-dad would feel about my faith. When he was younger, he had attended church sometimes, and he said that all the Christians he had ever known were hypocritical or judgmental. He said that people cried in church. He thought if Christianity was such a good thing, then it should make people happy.

Then we got our second miracle! While my step-dad was in prison, a preacher talked to him and invited him to a service. My step-dad went and asked God for forgiveness and accepted Christ into his heart.

At the same time God was also reaching out to my mom. One day at work, her friend told her about a small church. Her husband was the preacher, and she invited my mom to go. We visited the church. Cornelius, the pastor, didn't just preach the Word, he broke it down into small pieces so we could understand. I wanted to be there anytime the doors were open.

Today I'm sixteen years old. My step-dad is home from prison, and he's helping to minister in the small church we attend as a family. Recently, my mom was tested, and we received the best news. The doctor told her that she no longer had any evidence of Hepatitis C. I know what happened: My mom was healed!

When I was growing up, there were times when I thought that I was all alone. I'm sure my mom often thought that God had forgotten us, but my step-dad says it best. He says that God was with us the whole time, reaching out to us through other people, helping my family to find their way to Him.

I'm certainly living proof of that.

REAL SCRIPTURE

His purpose in all of this was that the nations should seek after God and perhaps feel their way toward him and find him—though he is not far from any one of us.

—ACTS 17:27 NLT

MY PRAYER

Dear Jesus, I know it wasn't Your plan for me to live this way. I realize that You grieve when You see someone like me hurting. I can't change my family. I can't change my circumstances, but I can allow You to live on the inside of me. I choose You, Christ. I will run after You no matter what I face. I believe that You will teach me and guide me and comfort me, that You will be my best Friend. I love You, Jesus. Thank You for walking with me through the tough times, and thank You for the better times ahead.

"I HAVE TO CHOOSE WHETHER I WANT TO LIVE WITH MY MOM OR MY DAD. MY CHOICE? MAKE THINGS LIKE THEY USED TO BE."

911

By Vicki M., Age 20

My world was rocked when my dad came into our bedroom that day. He held my sister and me close and said that he and mom were divorcing. It's hard to describe the pain when you're only eight years old and your parents say that they don't love each other anymore.

Things went downhill from that point forward. After Mom and Dad divorced, my mom dated her old high school boyfriend. He seemed okay in the beginning, but after they were married, we discovered that he had a drinking problem. He and my mother fought all the time. There were times when things flew through the air as they hurled items at each other. They were only married for a year.

The third marriage was to someone my mom met in a bowling alley. He also seemed nice in the beginning, but then he revealed his dark side. He drank quite a bit. He worked where alcohol was always available, and late at night he fought with my mom. This was worse than the previous marriage because now my mom was being physically abused.

One night he pushed her into the entertainment center, and the glass gashed deep cuts into her arms. She ran into my room, bleeding and saying that she wanted to die. My sister and I both witnessed many horrible scenes. I had to call for help many times. I was just a little kid, but I felt emotionally drained and damaged and very protective of my little sister.

It seemed like my mom gave up on herself. She tried to kill herself when things got really tough. She was depressed, and I didn't know what to do when she cut herself with razors or tied a hair dryer cord around her neck.

All I knew to do when things were out of control was to call 911. This became a familiar pattern. I called when Mom and her husband argued violently. I called when he threatened to hurt her. I called when her husband came after me with a butcher knife. Calling 911 meant that someone somewhere would hear me and come to my rescue.

My biggest fear was that one day it would be too late. That fear developed the night my stepfather cut the phone cord with a knife as I called. Luckily, the call had already made it through to the police.

To tell you the truth, I was afraid that every tomorrow would be worse than the day before. My only escape during that time was my every-other-weekend visit with my biological father. During those weekends, I could be a kid. It was wonderful, but then Monday always arrived.

I became my sister's protector. I didn't want her to see the abuse. I didn't want her in the middle of the arguments. It wasn't just the terrible fights, but also the questions that spun me in the middle of the battle: *Who do you think is right? Whose side are you taking anyway?* I didn't want that job, but I was still forced to take it.

The arguments made me heartsick, but I felt that if I could stand the pressure, my little sister wouldn't have to be a part of it. If I took the brunt, she wouldn't have to pay for the bad things that were happening to our family.

At night I cried myself to sleep. I stared at the ceiling, wondering why this was happening to my family. It didn't seem like things could get any worse, but then they did.

My sister and I were riding bikes down the street. A man in a blue station wagon sped around the corner. He wasn't paying attention, and by the time he saw my sister and me, it was too late to stop. The tires screeched, and the metal on the car scraped as it slammed into my sister's bike. She flew through the air backwards and landed on her back on the pavement. The car also hit my front tire, but I didn't even feel it. All I could think about was getting to my sister. I saw how badly she was hurt and screamed for someone to call 911. I ran as fast as I could toward a house and slammed into the patio doors, screaming for anyone to call for help.

Back at my sister's side, I could see that her knee and leg were at an awkward angle. As I held her hand, I wished that the car had crashed into me rather than her. She was only ten. Maybe it would have been different if the car had plowed into me.

My mother arrived at the same time as the ambulance, and I watched helplessly as the paramedics drove away with my mom and my broken and bruised sister.

My sister was in a hospital bed with a pin in her leg for the next three months. She seemed to be sick and in pain all of the time. I visited her every day, and my mom had to drag me away when visiting hours were over. My sister finally left the hospital in a partial body cast.

I was thrilled to have her home, but I struggled with my feelings of elation versus guilt. I felt like I had let my sister down because I was right by her when it happened. She was young and innocent, and I was supposed to protect her.

I had failed.

I became very depressed, and out of desperation one night, I decided to pray. I needed someone to help me. I had grown up with the knowledge of God and prayer, but I had never understood the greatness of it all. I had attended church before, but it always seemed cold rather than warm and inviting. I never doubted that God existed, but I didn't understand Him. Still, I asked Him for help anyway and hoped that He would hear me. It was Christmas time, and things were very bleak. My mom's third marriage had failed. It was a gloomy holiday as my mom tried her best to take care of us. There wasn't enough money to buy food or pay rent, much less celebrate Christmas.

There was a knock at the door. People from a local Christian church stood on the doorstep with food, clothes, and gifts. For no reason these people gave us a very special Christmas morning. I could hardly believe it. It seemed as if God had sent a message to me, telling me that He heard my prayer.

I started seeking God after that day. I was so used to taking care of things, being self-sufficient, and having no one to talk to, that the idea of finding a relationship with God stirred hope inside of me. I went to the church that had given us our Christmas surprise. I learned to pray and cry out to God, and soon I felt peace that I had never experienced before in my life. It seemed as if a huge weight was lifted off of my shoulders and that Someone was listening to me.

This had to be God!

Things slowly began to get better for my family. My sister went through months of physical therapy, and she is now well again. My mother met a new man, and our lives are blessed and normal. Even though my Mom and Dad's lives are not perfect, I know that God is always with me and that He loves me. Even when I feel so alone and it seems like there is nowhere to go, He is there for me to cast my cares on Him.

And when I do struggle, I still call 911—but this time it is a spiritual cry for help, and God answers me.

REAL QUOTE

If you could receive just a little taste of
what I've found as a Christian, then you would
want so much more. You're not alone. God can
help you no matter what you've gone through.

—BRANDON G., AGE 16

MY PRAYER

Dear Jesus, I am crying out for help. Sometimes
I don't know whom to trust, but I believe that
You will listen. Thank You for Your compassion,
not that You feel sorry for me, but that You move
toward me when You hear me cry. Thank You that
You are unchanging and that I can always trust You.

> *"I GUESS YOU CAN SAY I'M AN AGNOSTIC. PLEASE PRAY FOR ME BECAUSE IF THERE IS A GOD, I WANT TO KNOW."*

IF YOU ARE REAL . . .

By T. Suzanne Eller

The small church was crowded. All around me people worshiped a God Who I didn't believe existed. Why was I there? My neighbors had asked me to come, and, to be honest, I thought they would leave me alone after that if I did.

I wasn't sure what to expect. I had attended services with my family a few times, but it was more of a ritual or a way to celebrate holidays. What I hadn't anticipated was the wetness pressed against my eyelids as I clenched them shut.

My motto? Never let them see you cry. I wasn't about to break down in front of people I didn't know. I wasn't crying because I felt the presence of God or because I sensed His love for me. Rather, I fought tears because I was mad, so angry that I shook inside. How dare the preacher stand there and talk about the love of God! It was easy for him and people like him to spout off about a God who existed, who had a purpose for every person. Well, maybe their God had taken a personal interest in them, but He certainly didn't live at my house.

The mother I am about to share with you is not the same mom I have now. You see, she had an encounter with God, and He brought her out of the darkness of emotional pain and healed her. In order to share my story, I have to share a little bit of hers as well.

My mom left home at sixteen years old, pregnant and newly married to a boy who thought he was a man. She lost her first baby to cystic fibrosis when the toddler was less than two years old. She had her second child at eighteen, and she was abandoned by her husband at the age of twenty-one. He came to visit her one night and forced her to have sex. She discovered two weeks later she was pregnant.

I was that baby.

Mom married a good man who loved both her and the two little kids who came as a package deal. But in spite of this turn of events, my mom was fragile. Like stained glass, she was pretty on the

outside, but the broken pieces of her life created
the portrait.

Growing up, I never knew what to expect. Would
it be the mom who brought home suckers to surprise
us, or the woman who spouted, ran out the door, and
threatened to kill herself? These episodes were
always followed with tearful requests for forgiveness.

Please don't get me wrong. It wasn't always bad
in my home, but when it was, it was loud, chaotic,
and frightening. I feared one day that my mom would
pull the trigger or hurt herself. I hated the words that
came out of her mouth when she was angry.

One day my mom chased me through the house,
brandishing an umbrella as she screamed at me. I
ran out the door and into the rain. I was wearing a T-
shirt and jeans and no shoes. The cold rain pelted
me as I ran down Latimer Street. I pushed through
the wetness, pumping my arms and running as fast
as I could. Finally I stopped, bending down to catch
my breath as my tears meshed with the raindrops. I
slowly turned around, walked home, sat on the curb,
and wept until my throat closed.

I was stuck. I couldn't run away. I had no
money, no place to go. I was thirteen years old.
Where could I go?

I started smoking at the bus stop, pushing boundaries with my teachers, and drinking with my best friend. My attempts to be tough must have appeared hilarious to others. I was skinny to a fault and looked younger than my age. Being tough didn't come natural. My heart was gentle, and I hated conflict and fighting, yet every single time I let my guard down, someone hurt me.

Angry words all sharp and pointy, a knife in my soul.

That's when the hardness crept in. Never let them see you cry. Never give them a chance to know you care.

One day it all came to a head. My mom pulled us around her in her bedroom. She put a gun to her head and threatened to shoot herself. I was scared, not because I thought she would die, but because under my breath I whispered, "Just do it."

Who was this person I was becoming? I wondered.

My mom did not pull the trigger. I don't think she ever intended to, but instead was crying out for help. As a child, I had no way of recognizing that. Today I do.

Two years later I stood in the little church. The pastor sang, strumming on the guitar as people knelt at the altar. "He loves you," he said. "He has a plan for your life."

Yeah, right, I thought. I pointed my chin at the sky, eyes closed, and I challenged this God of whom he spoke. "If You are real," I whispered, "and I don't believe You are, but if You exist and You know me and You love me like he says, I need to know."

I expected nothing, yet I received everything as a tender touch reached past my hardened heart. I've had trouble explaining this moment to people over the years. "Did you see God?" No. "Did you feel God's presence?" Yes, but it was so subtle and deep inside of me, touching areas that I had closed long ago to everyone, that I knew it was God.

Tears broke and streamed down my cheeks, and for the first time in a long time I wept. I felt as if He had wrapped me in a warm blanket, enclosing me in His love. I stumbled from the church. I ran home and told my mom that I had just gotten "saved," though I really didn't understand what had occurred.

Did everything magically change? No. My circumstances were still the same, but everything was different on the inside of me.

I made mistakes, huge blunders, as I tried to learn what it meant to follow Jesus as my Savior. I wasn't perfect, but I understood His love. I knew that I wanted to know more. The people of that little church ministered to me in ways they will never understand. There were times when I wept at the altar and then went home to chaos. There were times when I fell in my walk with Christ, and their gentle encouragement helped me to keep going.

It is amazing what can happen when God restores a broken life. It can be beautiful like the portrait that my mom is now, the shattered pieces of her life assembled together in a beautiful picture of God's mercy.

Today I am a mom, an author, a speaker, and a wife. I have the opportunity to minister to teens and women across the nation, sharing the story of my life, the beauty of purpose, and the fact that God loves each of us so much. My mother and father were saved when I was in my junior year of high school. I found a note from my dad under my pillow one day. I still carry it with me, the tattered pieces are a reminder of what God has done. My quiet father, who very rarely shared the depth of his emotions, said in that letter, "I have watched you, and I see that you have something that is of great worth, a treasure. I know that it is real, and I admire you for your faith and your love for God."

We have never spoken of that letter, but it came at a time when I had prayed for a sign, saying, "God, show me that You hear my prayers. Heal my family. Let me know that You are listening." The folded piece of paper under my pillow was Heaven-sent and priceless.

For years my mom and I have been best of friends. She is compassionate, loving, and whole, and the memories of our past are forgiven and forgotten.

Today I am still running after the same God who touched my life when I was fifteen. I always tell my teen audiences that one day I'll be an old woman running after God with my walker. You see, He's done a million things for me. He's been with me through difficult times, but my love for Him will always be wrapped around that first moment when He reached down to an angry, hurting, skinny fifteen-year-old teenager and silently whispered that He loved me.

I still can't help but whisper back, "I love You too."

MY PRAYER

*Precious Father, You have amazed and delighted me
for twenty-eight years. It's hard to remember how lost
I felt the day I met You. These stories have reminded me
of how many times You have picked me up and gently
carried me through the tough times. Lord, I pray for
the teens who are reading this right now. Show them
that You are real. Let them feel You. Help them
understand Your tremendous love. Nurture them
as they take a step of faith toward You right now.
I thank You that You have destiny marked on their lives!*

TWISTED MAN

By T. Suzanne Eller

A twisted man in a twisted world,
Confused and worn by the twists of fate—
How did I get here and how do I leave
This tangled web I've come to hate?

An upright man with an uptight mind
Left him there still in his bind—
Can't you see you're a twisted man?
No time for you, I'm a busy man.

A simple Son with a simple plan
Gave His life for this one man,
Extended grace to the twisted soul
And turned his life around,

Placed his feet on a narrow path,
Four footprints in the sand,
Indented deep within the grains,
The young man's life in the palm of His hand.

"I'll guide you son, I'll renew your mind
Your life I claim, My love you'll find—"
A twisted man in a twisted world,
His heart made whole, the trap unfurled.

Now a righteous man in a twisted place
On a narrow path, he runs the race
To shout the news of the Son of Man,
An awesome God with a simple plan.

"He'll guide you, child. He'll renew your mind.
Your life He'll claim, His love to find.
I once was lost; my life was bound.
But now I'm saved; He turned me around."

One last message he must convey
To the upright man who's lost his way,
"The battle is real, the end is near
Stop playing church . . .

The cost is far too dear."

REAL RESOURCES

Abortion

- Unplanned Pregnancy.com—*http://www.unplanned-pregnancy.com/postabortion.php*—Post abortion helps.

Abuse

- Open Hearts Ministry—*http://www.gospelcom.net/openhearts/locations/*—Ministering to the abused through the love of Christ.

Campus Ministries

- Campus Crusade for Christ—*http://www.uscm.org/*—
- Chi Alpha—*http://www.chialpha.com/*—A movement of college students following Christ. Informal campus meetings, fellowship, and worship.
- Fellowship of Christian Athletes—*http://www.fca.org/*—Athletic ministry for athletes and coaches from middle school through professional.
- Intervarsity Christian Campus Fellowship—*http://www.gospelcom.net/iv/*—Evangelical campus mission serving on more than 560 college and university campuses nationwide.
- Student Venture—*http://www.studentventure.com/*—High school version of Campus Crusade.
- Youth Alive—*http://www.youth.ag.org/youth/yahome.cfm*—A ministry focused on presenting Jesus

Christ, the message of hope, to every student on every campus.

- Youth for Christ—*http://www.gospelcom.net/yfc/*—Junior High, High School, and Teens at Risk programs.

Counseling Helps

- 24 Hour Counselor—*http://www.lifeway.com/24hour/index2.htm*—Lifeway Christian Resources. Counselors share advice on 24 tough topics from unplanned pregnancies to a parent's abuse of drugs or alcohol.

- Dawson McAllister Hopeline—Personal counseling to age twenty-one or under, prayer and biblical reference. 972-580-8000. *http://www.teenhopeline.com/talk/index.html*—Live Interaction Center—Chat with a live adult prayer partner.

- I Need Help Right Now, a ministry of Missing Link—*http://misslink.org/help.html*—Tons of phone numbers, Web site addresses, and helps for numerous issues. Also lists practical helps at *http://misslink.org/practicl.html*

- Turning Point Ministries—423-899-4770 E-mail: tpoint@turningpointministries.org *http://www.turningpointministries.org/*—Call or e-mail for list of churches offering this ministry or go to: *http://www.turningpointministries.org/meeting_locations.html*

Devotions or Newsletters

- 850 Words of Relevant—*http://www.relevant-magazine.com/newsletter/*—Awesome weekly newsletter for young adults.

- Campus Journal—*http://www.gospelcom.net/rbc/cj/*— Daily online devotional for students.
- Real Teens, Real Faith—*http://groups.yahoo.com/ group/RealTeens_RealFaith*—T. Suzanne Eller's online monthly e-zine for teens. Real stories, quotes, poetry, devotions, and helps.
- Teen Light—*http://www.teenlight.com/*—Web site and e-zine written by and for teens.
- Truthwalk.com—*http://www.truthwalk.com/*—Weekly commentary on contemporary issues from a Christian perspective.
- Youthwalk Online—*http://www.gospelcom.net/iv/*— Evangelical campus mission serving on more than 560 college and university campuses nationwide.
- ZJAM Newsletter—*http://zjam.com/news/ index.html*—ZJAM Youth Ministries with Bill Scott and Dawson McAllister.

Discipleship, Training, and Youth Missions Programs

- Christian Discipleship—*http://www.christiandiscipleship.com/*—A safe place on the Internet where both young and mature Christians alike can receive spiritual nourishment through the Word of God.
- Master's Commission— *http://masterscommission.org/*—"A Generational Call to Character." A one-year Christian discipleship school with an emphasis on pursuing a passionate and effective relationship with Jesus Christ.
- Teen Mania—*http://www.teenmania.org/*—To initiate, facilitate, and sustain a massive movement of youth from all over the world for strategic short- and long- term missions.

- Teen Missions International—*http://www.teenmissions.org/*
- Youth with a Mission (YWAM)—*http://www.ywam.org/*— International movement of Christians working to help make a difference in a needy world.

Online Communities

- Campus Branch—*http://www.campusbranch.org/*
- Christian Teens. About.com— *http://christianteens.about.com/*—Led by Brandon Hill, thousands of teens interact in forums. Provides articles, book reviews, resources, music links, and more.
- Teen Mania—*http://www.teenmania.org/*— Online community and daily devotion.

Prayer Ministries

- 24/7 Prayer—*http://www.24-7prayer.com/*—Worldwide nonstop prayer movement for and by teens, designed to shape youth culture and bring teens back to the heart of Christ.

Pregnancy

- Bethany Christian Services— *http://www.bethany.org/*—Lifeline Pregnancy Hotline — 1-800-238-4269.
- Care Net Pregnancy Centers—*http://www.pregnantandscared.com/*—1-800-395-HELP (1-800-395-4357).
- Crisis Pregnancy Center Links Online—Find a pregnancy crisis center near you online.

- Unplanned Pregnancy.com—*http://www.unplanned-pregnancy.com/*—Caring solutions for the unplanned pregnancy.

Prostitution

- Children of the Night—*http://www.childrenofthenight.org/*—Rescuing teens and children from street prostitution—1-800-551-1300.

Runaway

- Covenant House—*http://www.covenanthouse.org/*—Call the "Nine Line" twenty-four hours a day/seven days a week—1-800-999-9999—Shelter and services to homeless and runaway youth.

Sexual Addiction/Pornography

- Exodus, Christian ministry to those who want freedom from homosexuality—*http://www.exodus-northamerica.org/findministry/*—Find a ministry near you.
- I Need Help Right Now—*http://misslink.org/help.html*—A site with helpful links to those struggling with pornography.
- Porn-Free.org—*http://www.porn-free.org/*—A site dedicated to helping people affected by sexual addictions.

Substance Abuse

- Alcoholics Victorious—*http://av.agrm.org/*—Directory of groups located in the United States.

- Teen Challenge Worldwide Network—
  http://www.teenchallenge.com/—Directory of Teen
  Challenge Centers in United States.
- Christians in Recovery—*http://www.christians-in-recovery.com/*—Over 1,800 pages of free information
  to help those struggling with recovery from sub-
  stance abuse.

Suicide

- Missing Link, Inc.—*http://misslink.org/distrib1.html*—Call the "Nine Line" twenty-four hours
  a day/seven days a week—1-800-999-9999—Shelter
  and services to homeless and runaway youth.

CONTRIBUTORS

Aaron A., p. 190, "Time Ran Out."

Champagne A., p. 100, "Backstabbers."
Champagne is a big part of the Manhattan Corps
Salvation Army church family. Her poetry has been
read to hundreds of teens at Salvation Army Teen
camps.

Alexandra A., p. 95, "Circle of Friends."

AnaLisha A., p. 83, "God's Mirror." AnaLisha is a
junior in high school and loves to be used of God in
prayer and reaching out to others who need a friend.

Darrin B., p. 28, "No Way Out." Darrin and Sarah
are college pastors at Destiny church in Ohio. They
hope to minister to the persecuted church as mis-
sionaries in the future.

Amanda B., p. 81, "Water Globe Dancer."

Lacynda B., p. 206, "Out of the Box." Lacynda is
an assistant youth leader and outreach coordinator
at the Church of God of Prophecy in Evansville,
Indiana.

Nathan B., p. 43, "I See Me." Nathan's true
passion is the Lord. He loves showing God his love
through words. Read more of Nathan's poetry at
www.puresoul.faithweb.com.

Tara B., p. 80, "Real Quote." Tara is a sophomore in high school and plans to be in ministry. She

competes in Ministry Fine Arts by preparing and sharing sermons with teens.

Will B., p. 27, "Real Quote."

Erin Danielle C., p. 144, "Seed, a Love Letter from God." Erin is a freshman in high school and continues to write poetry and grow in her love for God.

Jamie C., p. 64, "Strangers in My House." Jamie is a sophomore in high school. She is active in her youth group, Revolution, and in her discipleship class, Metamorphosis III. She says she is growing in God daily.

Annette Dammer is the publisher of We-eee! Writers' Ministries, Inc. Four "Real Quotes" on pages 36, 54, 99, and 186 were excerpted by permission from devotions found in *Meditation Warriors,* a teen2teen devotional written by teens of Fayetteville Christian school. For more information, visit *www.writersministries.com.*

Jody D., p. 110, "The Vile One."

Brittany D., p. 137, "Real Quote." Brittany would like to thank her family for giving her the courage to live for Christ. She would also like to thank her brother Tony and her pastor Richard Box.

Manny D., p. 115, "Hollow Man" and p. 124, "Hollow Man Lyrics." Manny and Marci now have a beautiful son, Zion Gabriel. Manny says that Zion is God's answer to the meaning of true innocence and purity. Go to *www.krisillis.com* for more information.

Natalie D., p. 45, "My Best Friend." Natalie is a junior nursing major attending Baylor University. Due to the experience with Jacob's near-drowning accident in 1996, she chose nursing as her career.

Melissa, E., p. 62, "Who Am I?" Melissa is a freshman at Southwestern Assembly of God University and plans to be a missionary to children in a persecuted nation.

Ryan E., p. 42, "Real Quote." Ryan is a freshman at Northeastern State University in Tahlequah, Oklahoma, and he plans to major in physical therapy.

Jennifer F., p. 134, "A Father's Love."

Jimmy G., p. 195, "Forever." Jimmy is a songwriter and vocalist in the five-member band FIRSTatLAST. For more information, visit *http://www.firstatlast.homestead.com*.

Brandon G., p. 213, "Living Proof," and p. 228, "Real Quote." Brandon is a junior in high school and is very involved in his church. He loves baseball and tinkering with his classic Mustang.

Meredith G., p. 109, "Real Quote."

Robert H., p. 138, "All Star." Robert is in youth ministry at South Hills Church Community. He is pursuing a Master of Divinity from Fuller Theological Seminary. Visit his Web site at *www.explode.org*.

Rebekah H., p. 52, "Sunrise." Rebekah is a seventeen-year-old senior. "Sunrise" was written in memory of her friend, Sarah. Her "Real Quote" was excerpted from *Meditation Warriors Devotions*.

Samantha H., p. 76, "Perfection Is Overrated." Samantha loves basketball and golf, and she enjoys singing.

Jennifer H., p. 169, "Surrender" p. 19, "Road to Recovery, and p.143 "Real Quote." Jennifer is pursuing a degree in psychology and is an active member of Faith Outreach Church. Her Web site is *www.threefeetdeep.net*.

Mike H., p. 178, "California Dreaming" and p. 188, "Divine Insomnia Rap." Mike is married to Becky, and they have a one-year-old son, Isaac. Mike is currently with the rap ministry, Real Eyes.

Stephanie H., p. 61, "Real Quote." Stephanie is a freshman at Central Bible College.

Nichole J., p. 69, "A Place to Call Home." Nichole is married to Bryan. They share in a ministry to help abused and neglected children through the court system.

Chad L., p. 163, "No Limits." Chad has traveled to China, Vietnam, and Cambodia sharing God's love and grace. He craves excitement and says he has found it serving God.

Penny Lent, p. 110, "The Vile One." Penny Lent is a columnist, editor, poet, artist, and publisher. She is a frequent speaker at schools and conferences. She is also a bungee jumper.

Cody M., p. 101, "Church Lady." Cody is pursuing Bible studies at Southwestern Assemblies of God University in Texas.

Lawrana M., p. 177, "The Cross."

Celine Marie F. M., p. 212, "If You Really Love Me." Celine was born in Manila, Philippines, and is a high school student who enjoys drawing, surfing the Web, and rollerblading.

Vicki M., p. 222, "911" and p. 92 "Real Quote." Vicki is twenty years old, resides in Fond du Lac, Wisconsin, and attends Community Church. She is currently pursuing a life of love and truth with Jesus Christ.

Kemisha N., p. 114, "Real Quote."

Erin P., p. 184, "Real Quote." Erin is a sophomore at Wingate University where she is studying neurobiology. Her quote was excerpted from a devotion published in *Meditation Warriors,* published by We-eee! Writers' Ministries, Inc.

Jacob P., p. 35, "P. K." and p. 194, "Real Quote." Jacob is striving to be more of a God chaser and hopes to move more into a role of ministry. He thanks his family and Crystal for their love and support.

Tommy R., p. 197, "Absolute Freedom." Tommy is earning his nursing degree and hopes to minister in medical missions.

Carrie R., p. 124, "Between My Two Worlds" and p. 133, "Senses." Carrie is a junior at Fort Gibson High School in Oklahoma.

David R., p. 36, "Real Quote." David is currently a freshman at Wingate University and plans to major in religion and philosophy. He is also a writer for *www.teenlight.org*. Quote excerpted from *Meditation Warriors Devotions*.

Nikki R., p. 87, "Trigger." Nikki is currently a missionary for the Harvest Army Church International in the Bronx.

Charity S., p. 51, "Real Quote."

Brooke S., p. 55, "Butterfly Man."

Laura S., p. 131, "Real Quote." Laura is a sixteen-year-old from Detroit. She is an active advocate for real and applied Christianity.

Shelly S., p. 99, "Real Quote." Shelly is a seventeen-year-old who enjoys dancing and making jewelry. She believes helping others is the best thing you can do in life.

Sandra S., p. 93, "Truth." Sandra says writing is her escape. She is involved in band, theater, and art.

Matt W., p. 152, "Real Quote."

Shana W., p. 153 "Our Little Family Secret" and p. 162 "Real Quote." Shana is married to Randy, and they serve as youth pastors. Shana and Randy have opened their home to love and nurture foster children.

Jessa W., p. 45, "Culture Shock."

Samantha Z., p. 171, "Tough Times."

ABOUT THE AUTHOR

T. Suzanne Eller is a popular
conference speaker to teens,
parents of teens, and women. She
has written about ministering to
teens for many publications,
including *Guideposts, Today's
Christian Woman, Pray!,* and her
own national newsletter, *Real
Teens, Real Faith.* Suzanne lives with her husband,
Richard, in Oklahoma. They are the parents of Leslie,
Ryan, and Melissa.

Suzanne invites your questions, thoughts, and
ideas. You can write her at <u>tseller@daretobelieve.org</u>,
or visit her web site at <u>www.daretobelieve.org</u>.

Additional copies of this book
and other titles published by RiverOak Publishing
are available from your local bookstore.

If you have enjoyed this book,

or if it has impacted your life,

we would like to hear from you.

Please contact us at:

RiverOak Publishing

Department E

P.O. Box 55388

Tulsa, Oklahoma 74155

Visit our Web site at:
www.riveroakpublishing.com